Public Relations Management

A Team-Based Approach

Diane F. Witmer

Kendall Hunt
publishing company

Cover image © Shutterstock, Inc.
Author image courtesy David W. Witmer

Kendall Hunt
publishing company

www.kendallhunt.com
Send all inquiries to:
4050 Westmark Drive
Dubuque, IA 52004-1840

Copyright © 2012 by Diane F. Witmer

ISBN 978-1-4652-0498-1

Printed in the United States of America
10 9 8 7 6 5 4 3 2 1

Contents

Acknowledgments

Many years ago, I was told that writing is a collaborative endeavor. That certainly is true in this case. Friends and colleagues have made suggestions, caught typos, tolerated my preoccupation with the manuscript, and generally cheered me on throughout the project. Dennis Gaschen, APR, Fellow PRSA; Lynda Hamilton; Doug Swanson, Ph.D., APR; and Coral Ohl, Ph.D., APR each provided invaluable suggestions. Jim Macnamara and Sandra Moriarty were both prompt and generous in responding to requests for information. Melinda Morgan Kartsonis, APR, Fellow PRSA and Stephen Gregg of Morgan Marketing & Public Relations, LLC contributed the sample public relations proposal for Golden Island Jerky, which incorporates input from Lynda Hamilton's Spring 2012 Cal State Fullerton Public Relations Management student teams: VACKS Public Relations; Modern Style Communications; CorePR; JAAMZ Public Relations, CruxPR; Poise Public Relations; Infinity Public Relations Agency; Quintette5 Consulting; CSUF Impact; and Tier One Public Relations. The designers and copyeditors at Kendall Hunt were extraordinarily patient and helpful, and Linda Chapman, my stellar production coordinator, promptly and good-naturedly guided me through the process from start to finish. Of course, my biggest thanks go to my incredibly supportive husband, Doug Millar, and my mother, Mary Witmer, for picking up the slack at home when I, all too often, forgot to make the coffee or feed the critters.

Introduction

It's finally happened. You've landed your first public relations assignment. Hooray! Then panic sets in. Questions whirl through your mind: How do I do this? What do I do first? What will best meet the client's needs? Use this book as a textual "deep breath." It offers answers to those questions, based on four simple premises: (1) trust the four-step public relations process, (2) take one step at a time, (3) strive for excellence, and (4) stay true to your ethical standards.

Terms Used In This Book

The following chapters outline what public relations is and does, discuss the importance of ethical communication, and provide guidance for preparing, executing, evaluating, and reporting the outcomes of a public relations plan. To develop a clear understanding of the public relations process, it is useful to agree on certain terms.

The Client

For our purposes, a *client* is a person or an organization for which you are working. If you are in a PR firm, you may work on accounts for many clients. If you work in a corporate or nonprofit environment, the client may be your primary employer. A client can be an individual or an organization; it can be an educational institution, a government agency, a multinational corporation, a small mom-and-pop shop, or a nonprofit organization. No matter what the context, though, the process of public relations is the same, and the ultimate goal is to establish and sustain beneficial relationships with and for the client.

Publics or Audiences?

This text uses the words *public* and *audience* interchangeably. Like definitions of public relations, definitions of publics or audiences vary widely. In the following chapters, both terms refer to groups of people who (1) share traits and/or interests and (2) can affect the wellbeing of a client. These groups may include stakeholders, who have some sort of vested interest in the organization.

Strategies, Tactics, and Tools

Strategies, tactics, and tools are widely used terms throughout the public relations profession, but their definitions vary, so a few words about them here will be helpful. Let's address the last of the three terms first.

For us, *tools* in public relations are the specific channels that are used to communicate with target publics. For example, your print media tools might be news releases, backgrounders, and media alerts, among other things. Novice practitioners often start thinking in terms of the tools they will use before they have done the research and planning that should undergird any program. Such a practice is sure to diminish the success of the project.

Tactics are the ways in which you communicate with target publics, and each tactic may include multiple tools. Examples of tactics are using print media or social media or town hall meetings or partnering with local businesses. It is often best to reach each target public using multiple tactics.

Finally, *strategies* tie the tactics together into a single, cohesive public relations program. Although multiple strategies might be appropriate when targeting highly disparate publics, it's best to have an overarching, unifying concept to give the overall program a consistent look and feel. For example, imagine that you are putting together a local public health education campaign for prevention of skin cancer. One of your key messages is encouraging people to wear sunscreen, and your target is teens and pre-teens. Although the key message is health related, health is not your best strategy to reach this young, appearance-conscious audience. Instead, you might look at ways to make wearing sunscreen trendy or "cool." One of your tactics might be the use of printed materials in local teen hangouts and shopping areas. The tools could include such items as posters, table tents, and point-of-sale brochures.

Media (and Nonmedia) Materials

Other terms that often are misused by beginners are press kits, press or media releases, pitches, and information packages. *Press release* is synonymous with *news release*. Which term you use is simply is a matter of preference and style.

As the name implies, *media alerts* are also sent to the media, but these are quick references, usually with bullet points outlining the five Ws and the H (who, what, why, where, when, and how). A "pitch" is the public relations person's first contact with a journalist or editor to propose or "pitch" a story idea, and it may be in the form of a phone call or a pitch letter.

A *press kit* is a packet (either digital or paper or both) of information that is sent specifically to the media. Typically, a press kit includes a news release, background-ers, fact sheets, and other materials that may be of use to journalists. Press kits are distributed only to the media, but you may assemble nearly identical bundles for other audiences, such as opinion leaders, stockholders, donors, or other stakeholders. In such cases, the materials are *not* press kits; they are *information packets*.

Chapter Overview

1. *Practicing Excellent and Ethical Public Relations*

   The first chapter refreshes the reader on the general purpose of public relations as a relationship-building communication function, discusses the importance of ethics in professional practice, and reviews the four-step process of public relations.

2. *Developing and Managing Effective PR Teams*

   This chapter addresses ways in which effective teams are formed, the difference between groups and teams, the stages of team development, and team management throughout a public relations project.

3. *Preparing and Proposing a Public Relations Plan*

   Chapter 3 outlines the general structure of a public relations plan and contextualizes it within the four-step public relations process. It then demonstrates how the plan can be incorporated into a formal proposal of work.

4. *Build It, But Will They Come? Persuasion, Creativity, & Newsworthiness*

   The fourth chapter discusses the importance of *content* and *creativity* in developing effective persuasive messages. It briefly describes a theory of persuasion and applies it to the development of message content. The chapter then explains how to develop creative ideas and how to incorporate newsworthiness into messages for the media.

5. *Writing the Public Relations Plan: Step 1 Research*

   This chapter explains the importance of both formative and evaluative research for public relations planning and in evaluation of program effectiveness. Primary and secondary research tools for audience analysis, situation analysis, organizational analysis, and assessment also are discussed.

6. *Writing the Public Relations Plan: Step 2 Planning*

   Chapter 6 takes a Management by Objectives (MBO) approach and describes the criteria and writing of effective goals and objectives. It draws connections between well-written objectives and program management tools, including calendar, budget, and program evaluation techniques.

7. *Writing the Public Relations Plan: Step 3 Implementation*

   The seventh chapter explicates how the implementation phase of a public relations program should be described in a PR plan, including appropriate content and format for effective and accurate calendars and budgets.

8. *Writing the Public Relations Plan: Step 4 Evaluation*

   This chapter draws on the research concepts that are outlined in Chapter 5 to describe the ways in which objectives are measured for overall assessment of program success.

9. *Reporting the Public Relations Program Results*

   Chapter 9 outlines the final report of a public relations program, including organization of materials and drawing appropriate conclusions.

10. *Preparing and Delivering Professional Presentations*

    This chapter addresses preparation, structure, and timing of formal business presentations. Topics include development and use of effective visual aids and appropriate dress.

Additional Materials In This Text

Beyond the 10 chapters, this text includes nine appendices, a glossary of terms, and an index of important concepts and names. The first seven appendices are statements from major professional organizations concerning ethical standards.

Appendices 8 and 9 show two forms of a full public relations proposal. The first form is the proposal as it might appear when sent to a potential client. In this case, it is a proposal from Morgan Marketing and Public Relations, LLC, which has been accepted by the client, Golden Island Gourmet Snacks. The second form is an annotated version that identifies each element of the plan as outlined in Chapter 3.

Chapter 1
Practicing Excellent and Ethical Public Relations

It is not true, as some writers assume in their treatises on rhetoric, that the personal goodness revealed by the speaker contributes nothing to his power of persuasion; on the contrary, his character may almost be called the most effective means of persuasion he possesses.

~ Aristotle

This chapter refreshes the reader on the general purpose of public relations as a relationship-building communication function, describes key theories that inform public relations practices, discusses the importance of ethics in professional practice, and reviews the four-step public relations process.

LEARNING OBJECTIVES:

The information presented in this chapter will enable you to:

1. Describe public relations as a form of communication that establishes and maintains relationships.

2. Define organizations as social systems.

3. Identify key elements of the communication process using traditional models of communication.

4. Explain Grunig and Hunt's four models of public relations.

5. Define ethics and discuss key ethical imperatives for public relations.

6. Outline the four-step public relations process.

As you contemplate developing a public relations plan, it's important to keep in mind the underlying purpose of public relations. Without a clear vision of what PR is and does, it's impossible to develop an effective and cohesive public relations plan. Ultimately, you run the risk of boxing yourself into the role of technician, rather than that of strategist.

There are nearly as many definitions of public relations as there are practitioners. These definitions often focus on the activities and tools of public relations, such as publicity or dissemination of messages, rather than the overarching purpose of PR. While such ideas are not wrong, per se, they are incomplete and inadequately address the implications and significance of public relations.

Public Relations: The Emphasis Is on *Relationships*

In this text, we adopt the perspective of public relations as a specialized form of communication that manages relationships. This concept emphasizes outcomes, rather than activities, and promotes thinking conceptually, rather than tactically. As public relations practitioners, we build professional relationships with many organizations and many people, including clients, clients' target publics, media, vendors, and employees. The primary purpose of public relations, then, focuses on the management of professional relationships among organizations or individuals and their target publics.

Cutlip, Center, and Broom (1994, p. 2) perhaps phrased it best by stating that public relations is "the management function that establishes and maintains mutually beneficial relationships between an organization and the publics on whom its success or failure depends." The idea of establishing and maintaining mutually beneficial relationships underscores a give-and-take approach to public relations, rather than one of pure message dissemination and persuasion. In other words, PR is a form of communication that aims to establish *dialogs* with target publics, not simply create and distribute messages to them. Public relations also is most effective when practiced as a management function. Certainly, strategic planning and organizational decisions should consider such basic public relations interests as opinions, attitudes, and behaviors of all internal and external publics that can potentially affect organizational health.

Public relations is "the management function that establishes and maintains mutually beneficial relationships between an organization and the publics on whom its success or failure depends."

(Cutlip, Center, & Broom, 1994, p. 2)

Since public relations typically is practiced for or within organizations, we need to think a bit about the interdependence among organizations and their internal audiences, their external audiences, and their environments. One of the most useful ways to do this involves systems theory (von Bertalanffy, 1968), which undergirds many public relations models.

Systems Theory in a Nutshell

Thinking of organizations as *systems* allows us to account for complex behaviors of and relationships between internal and external entities. Systems are generally defined as interrelated sets of elements that create a unique, bounded whole. Systems function within the contexts of their surroundings or environments, and they're categorized according to their relative openness to environmental influences.

Closed systems are, as the name implies, functionally unresponsive to environmental stimuli. An example of a closed system is your wristwatch. Within its functional limits, it neither recognizes nor adjusts to heat or cold or spatial orientation. As long as the mainspring is wound or the battery is charged, it simply keeps on ticking.

Open systems, on the other hand, are sensitive to environmental factors, and they respond and adjust to achieve and maintain *homeostasis* or internal balance. These systems also use resources from the environment as *input*, transform those resources during a process we call *throughput*, and produce an *output* of some sort. A rose bush, for example, uses sunlight to photosynthesize moisture and nutrients from the soil to produce energy for growth, reproduction, and discharge of oxygen. The nutrients, moisture, and sunlight constitute input, photosynthesis is the throughput, and growth, reproduction, blossoms, and oxygen are outputs. The bush is sensitive to its environment, and it contains internal mechanisms that allow it to adapt to environmental change.

Although open and closed systems seem to be two discrete types, they actually are two ends of a continuum, and systems exhibit varying degrees of openness along that continuum. Regardless of the extent to which they're open or closed, though, all systems share certain features. First, they are comprised of interrelated elements or components that work together, often in complex ways, to support system function. Second, they are delineated by discrete *boundaries* within which the components interact. Third, systems are *hierarchical*. This means that systems work together with other systems as components of larger *suprasystems*, and that their components, in turn, are *subsystems* (see Figure 1-1, adapted from Athey, 1982).

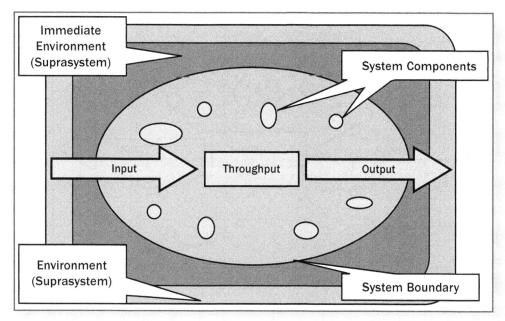

FIGURE 1-1
This diagram of a simple system shows a variety of system components, which interact to transform input into system output. A boundary defines the system within its immediate environment.

The hierarchical arrangement of systems renders system identification relatively arbitrary. Looking again at our rose bush, we can see veins in the leaves, which are part of a circulatory system that is bounded by vessel walls and encompasses interconnected components, such as cells and fluids. Here, then, because we are looking at the circulatory system, the rose bush becomes the immediate environment or suprasystem, and the cells become subsystems. Furthermore, the cellular systems contain yet more subsystems (for example organelles, such as mitochondria, ribosomes, and nuclei) that interact to process resources for such system functions as cellular reproduction.

Organizations as Social Systems

Although we've so far explored the basic concepts of systems theory in terms of the natural sciences, the concept of systems is widely used in the social sciences. Organizations can be viewed as *social systems*. Here, system components may be defined as individual people or organizational departments or even campuses of a large university. The input may be raw materials that are processed to yield manufactured goods or financial resources that are processed to support research. Organizations of any size or purpose are socially constructed through human interactions and are, therefore, social systems.

Social systems are delineated by permeable boundaries (Stohl, 1995). A consideration of people as organizational system components provides a clear example of this concept. Human beings live, work, and play in a multitude of social systems. We join churches, go to schools, work in businesses, and socialize in clubs. In each case, we influence the characteristics and cultures of those social systems, even as they influence us.

From a systems perspective, public relations functions as both system component and boundary spanner (probably first described by Aldrich & Herker in 1977). The PR practitioner, illustrated in Figure 1-2 (adapted from Athey, 1982), brings information into the organization and sends information back into the environment.

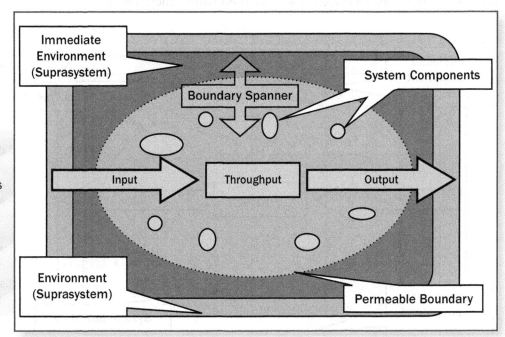

FIGURE 1-2
The role of public relations as boundary spanner in a social system. Note the permeable boundary.

Since public relations is a communications undertaking that serves boundary-spanning in organizations, we need to explore the process by which all this happens. That means some discussion of the process of communication is in order.

Understanding the Process of Communication

There are many models of communication, dating back to Aristotle's identification of source, message, and destination, but we consider only a few that are particularly helpful for understanding the practice of public relations. The first is Harold Lasswell's (1948) description of the process, which he summarized in a few simple words:

Who [says] *What* [through] *which Channel* [to] *Whom* [with] *What Effect?*

Lasswell's idea was that a communicator ("who") sends a message ("what") through some sort of medium ("channel") to a message receiver ("whom"), and that the communication results in some sort of effect. A one-way mathematical model developed by Claude Shannon and Warren Weaver (1949), which is shown in Figure 1-3, provides a nice visualization of this concept and adds new concepts.

This model depicts an *information source* that produces a message; a *transmitter* (or sender) that converts the message into a communicable *signal*; environmental *noise*, which disrupts the signal; a *receiver* that reconstructs the message from the signal; and the *destination* or recipient of the message. Shannon and Weaver were looking at information technology and the conversion of messages into electronic signals, but their general ideas can be translated into cognitive processes. Of course, this linear approach does not fully characterize the process of communication, but it does give us a start on developing a communication vocabulary.

FIGURE 1-3 The Shannon and Weaver Model of Communication illustrates one-way communication with no feedback loop.

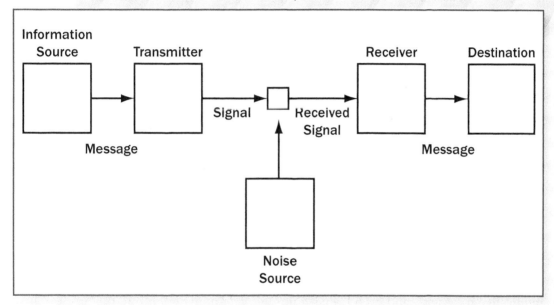

FIGURE 1-4 Wilbur Schramm incorporated a psychological frame of reference into the communication model. This recognized that the "field of experience" is unique for each message sender and for each receiver, and that communication can occur only where commonalities lie.

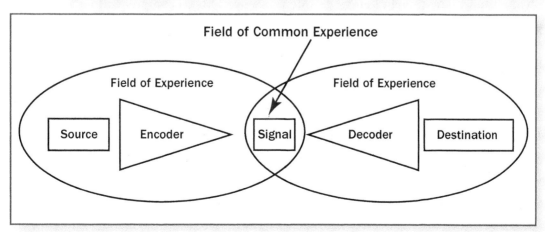

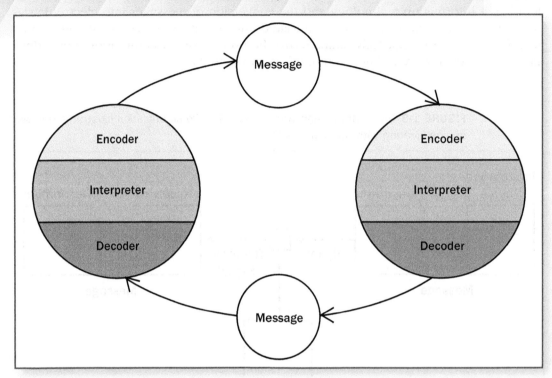

A more sophisticated model was developed by Wilbur Schramm (1954), which considers communication as a two-way process (see Figure 1-4). Here, both the message sender and message receiver are fully engaged in producing and transmitting communicative messages, and each brings a unique *field of* experience to the process. It is within the *field of common experience* that communication occurs.

The circular Osgood and Schramm (see Schramm, 1954) model of communication (Figure 1-5), still widely used, shows both the message sender and the message receiver as *interpreters* that encode messages they are sending and decode messages they are receiving. This model denotes the dicey problem of creating meaning through symbols and how human beings decode those symbols to comprehend meaning.

Admittedly, the models described here are limited, in that they are flat, two-dimensional representations of intricate multilevel processes. They cannot address the complexities of multiple senders, messages, receivers, and feedback loops in today's technological world. Many more sophisticated models, which assume nonlinear and multidimensional perspectives, attempt to explore the complexities of communication. Some even use holographic and fractal methodologies. However, the two-dimensional models described above do provide a basis for discussion and a foundation for considering contemporary models and processes of public relations.

Perhaps the most robust models that address the various ways in which PR is practiced are the four models that were developed by James Grunig and Todd Hunt in 1984. In brief, these four models, summarized in Table 1-1, follow an evolutionary approach to the practice of public relations, and they are categorized as one-way or two-way communication.

TABLE 1-1: Grunig & Hunt's Four Models Of Public Relations

	One-Way Communication		Two-Way Communication	
Distinguishing Characteristic	Press Agentry/ Publicity	Public Information	Two-Way Asymmetrical	Two-Way Symmetrical
Nature of Communication	Persuasion & Manipulation	Objective Information Dissemination; Persuasion	Scientific Persuasion; Propaganda	Dialogic Communication
Ethical Perspective	Truth Not Essential	Truth Important	Truth Important	Truth Essential
Research Used	Almost None: "Counting House" (Press Clippings, etc.)	Little: Readability & Readership	Formative Methods & Evaluative of Attitudes & Behaviors	Formative Methods & Evaluative of Understanding, Attitudes, & Behaviors
Key Historical Figures	P. T. Barnum	Ivy Ledbetter Lee	Edward L. Bernays	Normative Theory
Area Typically Practiced	Sports & Entertainment; Product Promotion	Government; Nonprofit; Organizations; Businesses	Businesses; Agencies	Regulated Businesses; Agencies

Adapted from Grunig & Hunt, 1984, p. 22.

One-Way Communication Models

1. **One-Way Asymmetrical Model of Communication**: Also known as the *Press Agentry Model*, this is the earliest form of public relations, and perhaps the one that still tends to jump into people's minds when they think of PR. Press agentry uses persuasion and manipulation to influence and control target publics. It is not concerned with truth and accuracy or with audience feedback, and it is not based on formative research. Rather, it takes a "counting house" approach of simply counting such things as the number of products sold or how many people attended an event. American showman P. T. Barnum was a master at this form of public relations during the late 19th century. Press Agentry is most easily observed in the entertainment industry and product promotion (think "miracle" diet drugs!).

2. **One-Way Symmetrical Model of Communication**: This is often called the *Public Information Model*. It differs from the press agentry model in that truth and accuracy are important. However, the information is selectively disseminated, and this form of PR relies on very little research other than measuring readability and readership. Ivy Ledbetter Lee's image restoration of John D. Rockefeller Sr. is a classic example of the one-way symmetrical model.

   On April 20, 1914, the Colorado National Guard attacked striking coal miners in Ludlow, Colorado. Nineteen people, including two women and 11 children, died in the encounter. John D. Rockefeller, who founded Standard Oil, was already a controversial figure (see Figure 1-6 for a disparaging cartoon dated long before the Ludlow incident), in part because of "muckraker" journalist Ida Tarbell's public attacks on him and the Standard Oil "robber barons" of the day.

FIGURE 1-6 "The Infant Hercules and the Standard Oil Serpents" by Frank A. Nankivell first appeared in *Puck* magazine, May 23, 1906. The image depicts U.S. President Theodore Roosevelt as the "Infant Hercules" grappling with Standard Oil "serpents" John D. Rockefeller (r) and Nelson W. Aldrich (l).

THE INFANT HERCULES AND THE STANDARD OIL SERPENTS.

FIGURE 1-7 Edward L. Bernays (1891–1995) in the early 1920s. Bernays was a double nephew of Sigmund Freud and applied Freudian concepts to public relations.

Since the Ludlow mine was part of the Rockefeller-owned Colorado Fuel & Iron Company, the massacre further damaged his reputation. Ivy Lee used a variety of strategies to soften Rockefeller's public image and to bring to public attention his historic, but largely unknown philanthropic accomplishments. The public information model continues to be widely practiced in government agencies and nonprofit organizations.

Two-Way Communication Models

3. **Two-Way Asymmetrical Model of Communication:** This model is based on social scientific theories and methods, including research. It is sometimes called *Scientific Persuasion*. Here, practitioners both gather information from and provide it to target publics, using social scientific methods. While this model incorporates audience feedback into communications, the feedback is used to develop more persuasive strategies, rather than to meet audience needs.

Edward L. Bernays (1891-1995) was among the first to apply social scientific methods to the practice of public relations. In the early 20th century, he codified those techniques in his groundbreaking text *Crystallizing Public Opinion* (1929). Bernays considered propaganda a necessity in a democratic society, but liked to say that he practiced "propaganda, not impropaganda" (Blumer & Moyers, 1984). Corporate public relations often follows this model.

4. **Two-Way Symmetrical Model of Communication:** This is a *normative* model; in other words, it proposes an ideal, rather than a description of typical practice, and it holds the most potential for true excellence in public relations. The two-way symmetrical model relies on social scientific research methods and emphasizes a true dialog between organizations and their publics. This means that listening to those publics is a critical aspect of effective public relations. Here, feedback is not only used to develop persuasive strategies, but to promote mutual understanding. Of course, truth and accuracy are of utmost importance.

Kent State Associate Professor Bill Sledzik, Ph.D., APR, Fellow PRSA blogs:

> Today's amoral, profit-lusting business environment doesn't leave much room for the 2-way symmetrical model, which, by definition, may not be self-centered. Makes it hard to justify shareholder greed and 7-figure bonuses when you have to worry about fairness, balance and the whole "relationship" thing.

> Can public relations move American business toward a more balanced business model and a more ethical one? Maybe not. But someone has to try.

Reprinted with permission.

The concepts of truth, accuracy, and audience manipulation are fraught with ethical dilemmas, and all four of the Grunig and Hunt models of communication carry with them ethical implications. Every day, public relations professionals are faced with making ethical choices—sometimes tough choices. Thus, a brief discussion of ethics is in order.

Ethics in Public Relations

Like public relations itself, the term *ethics* has a variety of definitions, but in broad-brush terms, ethics is a branch of philosophy that addresses such concepts as good and evil, right and wrong, and other issues of morality. In applied ethics, such as practicing ethical public relations, we are concerned with professional standards of conduct. This is a critical concept for PR practitioners, for three key reasons:

1. Public relations practitioners can find themselves in situations that divide loyalties. While journalists typically have a responsibility to serve the general public, PR professionals are advocating for a client. This can lead to a variety of challenging dichotomies. What, for example, does one do if the client who is paying the practitioner has goals that are not in the best interests of the general public? It is easy to *say* that the PR person, although an advocate for the client, must be socially responsible, but that is not always easy in practice.

2. Public relations often involves such powerful strategies as mass media, social media, personal networking, and the printed word. Practitioners must be mindful of this power, recognize the potential for manipulation of public opinion, and consider potential unintended consequences of their plans before implementation. This means research and thought should precede action.

3. Public relations as a profession, ironically, continues to labor under the weight of the press agentry model and struggles with its own image management. Terms like "spin doctor" and "flack" continue to permeate the business world, and practitioners struggle to rehabilitate the public image of PR as a high-quality, reputable profession. The problem is perpetuated, in part, by the ethical conundrums described above. Thus, the burden is squarely on today's practitioner to be above reproach in all professional dealings.

To address these concerns, nearly all organizations involved with PR, including Public Relations Society of America (PRSA), International Association of Business Communicators (IABC), American Marketing Association (AMA), Institute for Advertising Ethics (IAE), International Public Relations Association (IPRA), and the United Kingdom-based Chartered Institute of Public Relations (CIPR), have formal codes of ethics that proscribe inappropriate practices. Although there are distinct differences among the codes, some general commonalities do exist. First, the PR practitioner is challenged to find opportunities and solutions that will serve the greater good as well as the client when there is a disparity between the two. Second, honesty, integrity, truth, and accuracy must be practiced in all undertakings at all times. Third, the PR professional should treat all audiences, including past and current clients and employers, with fairness, dignity, and respect. (For full copies of the PRSA, IABC, AMA, AAF, IPRA, and CIPR codes of ethics, refer to Appendices 1 through 6 at the end of this textbook.)

The Arthur W. Page Society, named for the 1927–1946 American Telephone and Telegraph Company (AT&T) vice president of public relations, is a membership organization of senior professionals that stresses high ethical standards. The society publishes "The Page Principles" on its website, which summarize a focus on excellent and ethical public relations. (These seven principles appear in Appendix 7 at the end of this textbook.) Of course, practicing public relations in alignment with Grunig and Hunt"s Two-Way Symmetrical Model of Communication helps make these ideals possible.

As discussed earlier, the two-way symmetrical model of communication constitutes a dialog between the client and its target publics. As with any dialog, well-practiced PR involves listening. To do that, we must first understand who our target publics are, who and what influence them, what environmental pressures they face, what they value, what they disvalue, how they spend their time and resources, and what they watch, listen to, and read. Understanding those things allows us to find ways in which we can reach our target publics, both to gather information and to provide it. Of course, successfully targeting publics involves research, the first step of the four-step public relations process. Public relations research is outlined in some detail in Chapter 5. In this chapter, we review the general process.

The Four-Step Public Relations Process

Communication, including public relations, is not a one-time event. It is an ongoing, iterative process. In the field of public relations, the process is generally broken down into four interrelated and repetitive steps. Various acronyms are used to describe the four steps, with RACE and ROPE, shown in Table 1-2, being two of the most popular. Although the specific terms used to describe the process differ somewhat among scholars and practitioners, the basic concepts are the same. We adopt the general language of the PRSA. Thus, the four steps of the public relations process are:

TABLE 1-2: The Four-Step Public Relations Process

	Acronym: RACE	Acronym: ROPE	PRSA Language
?	**R**esearch	**R**esearch	Research
◎	**A**ction Planning	**O**bjective Setting	Planning
!	**C**ommunication	**P**rogramming	Implementation
?	**E**valuation	**E**valuation	Evaluation

1. ⑦ **Research**: Gathering pertinent information about the client, environmental factors, the client's industry, the target publics, the product or service, economic forecasts, and other data to inform the PR plan and make strategic decisions.

2. ◎ **Planning**: Establishing goals and objectives, timelines, budgets, implementation strategies, tools, tactics, and methods that will be used to evaluate program success. Continuing research as necessary.

3. ① **Implementation**: Putting the plan into action, continuing to gather information, implementing the tactics that were laid out in Step 2, Planning.

4. ② **Evaluation**: Measuring program success in terms of the stated objectives. Often requires research methods used in Step 1, Research.

While every step of the process appears discrete, all four steps are iterative. We revisit and refine each step as we move through the process. For example, although research is the first step, it's not something we do and set aside. We conduct research throughout an entire project, and it is never really *finished*. New questions arise throughout the process, and the answers require more research. In fact, the evaluation of one program often becomes part of the research step for repetitive or similar programs in the future. We also use research methods in the evaluation step, and sometimes evaluative research, such as survey studies to measure changes in audience awareness or attitude, must be started before a plan is implemented. For these reasons, it's helpful to think of research and evaluation as matching "bookends" to the public relations plan.

Tying It All Together

This chapter presented foundational information and context for the effective and ethical practice of public relations. It described public relations as a communication function that establishes and manages relationships between a client and its target publics. This approach places the focus on outcomes, rather than on tools and tactics, and it requires us to understand the interrelationships between clients and their target publics. A systems perspective helps us understand the complexities of those relationships and places public relations in a boundary-spanning role that bridges internal and external organizational communications.

The chapter described several basic models of communication, which, although limited, provide a conceptual language for describing and practicing public relations.

Grunig and Hunt"'s four models of public relations were briefly outlined: Press Agentry/ Publicity, Public Information, Two-Way Asymmetrical, and Two-Way Symmetrical. Each model describes a way in which public relations currently is practiced, and each brings with it ethical implications. This led us to briefly explore ethics and to identify some concepts common to many professional codes of ethics. Having established a conceptual and ethical framework for the practice of public relations, this chapter previewed the four-step public relations process, which is addressed in depth in chapters 5, 6, 7, and 8.

Name _____Date _____

REFLECT AND REVIEW

1. Based on what you have learned in this chapter, define public relations in your own words.

   _____

   _____

   _____

2. Think of an organization in which you work or play. Consider it as a social system and label each of the elements in the diagram below.

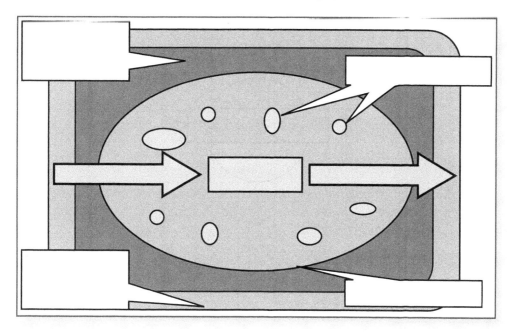

3. Keeping in mind your answer from #2 above, consider the communications in which this organization is engaged. Identify one target public and messages, and then label all the shaded boxes in the model.

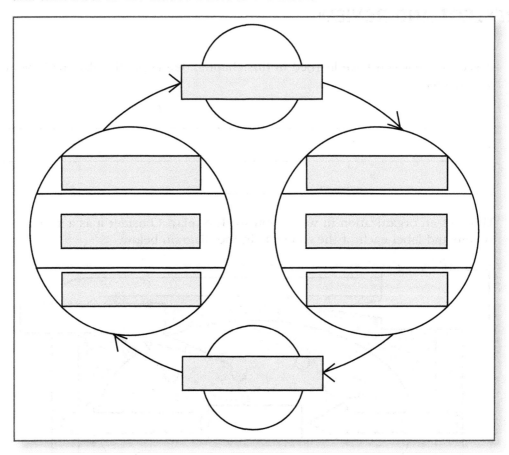

4. Reflect on Grunig and Hunt's four models of public relations. How much of the table below can you complete?

Grunig & Hunt's Four Models Of Public Relations

	One-Way Communication		Two-Way Communication	
	Press Agentry / Publicity	Public Information	Two-Way Asymmetrical	Two-Way Symmetrical
Distinguishing Characteristic				
Nature of Communication				
Ethical Perspective				
Research Used				
Key Historical Figures				
Area Typically Practiced				

5. Define ethics and name three key ethical imperatives for public relations that span the several codes of ethics.

   Ethics is: _____

   _____

   1. _____

   2. _____

   3. _____

6. Briefly describe the four-step public relations process.

   1. _____

   2. _____

   3. _____

   4. _____

CHAPTER 1 REFERENCES AND RESOURCES

Aldrich, H., & Herker, D. (1977). Boundary spanning roles and organization structure. *The Academy of Management Review, 2*(2), 217–230.

Aristotle. (n.d.). *Rhetoric*, Book 1, Chapter 2, 1356a. Retrieved from http://rhetoric.eserver.org/aristotle/rhet1-2.html#1356a

Aristotle. (c. 335–323 BCE). *The metaphysics* (Book VIII, Part 6). New York: Cosimo.

Aristotle, & Freese, J. (1959). *The "Art" of Rhetoric.* Cambridge, Mass.: Harvard University Press

Athey, T. H. (1982). *Systematic systems approach: An integrated method for solving systems problems.* Englewood Cliffs, NJ: Prentice-Hall.

Bernays, E. L. (1929). *Crystallizing public opinion.* New York: Liveright.

von Bertalanffy, L. (1968). *General systems theory.* New York: Braziller.

Blumer, R., & Moyers, B. (1984). *A walk through the twentieth century with Bill Moyers: The image makers* [video]. College Park, MD: Corporation for Entertainment & Learning, Inc.

Cutlip, S. M., Center, A. H., & Broom, G. M. (1994). *Effective public relations.* Englewood Cliffs, NJ: Prentice-Hall.

Grunig, J. E. (Ed.). (1992). *Excellence in public relations and communication.* Hillsdale, NJ: Lawrence Erlbaum Associates.

Grunig, J. E., & Hunt, T. (1984). *Managing public relations.* New York: Holt, Rinehart & Winston.

Grunig, L. A., Grunig, J. E., & Dozier, D. M. (2002). *Excellent public relations and effective organizations: A study of communication management in three countries.* Mahwah, NJ: Lawrence Erlbaum Associates.

Kent, M. L., & Taylor, M. (2002). Toward a dialogic theory of public relations. Public Relations Review, *28*, 21–37.

Lasswell, H. D. (1948). *Power and personality.* New York: W. W. Norton.

Ledingham, J. A., & Bruning, S. D. (Eds.). (2000). *Public relations as relationship management: A relational approach to the study and practice of public relations.* Mahwah, NJ: Lawrence Erlbaum Associates.

Nankivell, F. (1906, May 23). *The infant Hercules and the Standard Oil serpents*. Washington, DC: The Library of Congress, Prints and Photographs Division. Retrieved from http://www.theodorerooseveltcenter.org/Research/Digital-Library/Record.aspx?libID=o278539

Schramm, W. (1954). How communication works. In W. Schramm (Ed.), *The process and effects of mass communication*. Urbana, IL: University of Illinois Press.

Shannon, C. E., & Weaver, W. (1949). *The mathematical theory of communication*. Urbana, IL: University of Illinois Press. (Reprinted with corrections from *The Bell System Technical Journal, 27* (July, October, 1948), 379–423, 623–656.

Sledzik, W. E. (2008, August 10). *The '4 Models' of public relations practice: How far have you evolved?* [Blog]. Retrieved from http://et.kent.edu/toughsledding/?p=969

Stohl, C. (1995). *Organizational communication: Connectedness in action*. Thousand Oaks, CA: SAGE Publications.

Chapter 2
Developing And Managing Effective PR Teams

The way a team plays as a whole determines its success. You may have the greatest bunch of individual stars in the world, but if they don't play together, the club won't be worth a dime.

~ Babe Ruth

This chapter addresses the difference between groups and teams, the ways in which effective teams are formed, the stages of team development, and team management throughout a public relations project.

LEARNING OBJECTIVES:
The information presented in this chapter will enable you to:

1. Distinguish between teams and groups.

2. Identify similarities and differences between you and potential teammates.

3. Describe five stages of team life cycles.

4. Establish team standards and conduct efficient team meetings.

5. Manage team processes and conflicts.

At first glance, a chapter on team management may seem a little odd in a public relations text, but teamwork is an integral part of PR. Whether you work in a public relations firm or within a single "client" organization, chances are you will develop and execute public relations plans in cooperation with others. Devine and Clayton (1999) noted that most companies of 100 or more employees use teams in some form, and a 2011 study by the National Association of Colleges and Employers reported that the ability to work in a team was the #1 soft skill employers looked for on a résumé and in job interviews. To give you an idea of the extent to which teamwork pervades PR, a quick Google search for "public relations team" as this text was being written yielded about 67,400 results in 0.20 seconds.

It's not a stretch to understand the advantages of teams. We know intuitively that we can accomplish things in cooperation with others that we cannot accomplish alone. Years of study have been invested in trying to understand the intricacies of team formation, development, productivity, and leadership. This text touches on a few key ideas that may help you through the process of putting together and managing effective teams. First, though, let's make sure we understand what constitutes a team.

Teamwork or Groupwork?

The terms *team* and *group* are often used interchangeably, but there are some generally agreed-on differences. Although all teams are groups, not all groups are teams. The differences lie primarily in the members' goals and processes.

Katzenbach and Smith (1993) provide us with an excellent definition of a *team* as "a small group of people with complementary skills who are committed to a common purpose, performance goals and approaches for which they are held mutually accountable" (p. 112). In contrast, groups are composed of people who may or may not have a common goal, work as individuals to achieve group goals, are not equally invested in the outcome, and do not necessarily share the same standards of performance. The classic example of a group is that of a jury. Here, 12 individuals with disparate values, motivations, backgrounds, knowledge bases, and experiences are charged with a goal of reaching agreement on a verdict. Although a verdict may be determined, jury members typically work individually, do not rely on each other's unique talents, may have difficulty resolving conflict, and have unequal levels of commitment.

In contrast to groups, teams are typically characterized by a shared vision, internal cooperation, and group cohesion. Team members recognize and rely on each other's unique talents and skills to accomplish tasks and share responsibilities. Consider, for example, a surgical team. Each member has a unique role, a specific set of skills, a shared commitment to the goal of a successful surgery, and trust in each other that individual duties will be accomplished. The goal, then, in public relations is to form strong, cohesive *teams* rather than groups. In fact, the real aim is to form *synergistic* teams.

FIGURE 2-1 Just as individual fingers work in cooperation to accomplish tasks, individual team members must work in concert to accomplish team goals.

© istockphoto.com

Synergistic Teamwork

Synergism, derived from the Greek word synergós (ΣΥΝΕΡΓΌς), typically refers to components or agents working together to create a magnified outcome or entity. The classic definition of synergy, drawn from Aristotle's *Metaphysics* (Book VIII, Part 6), is phrased as "the whole is more than the sum of its parts." One simple example of synergy can be found in pharmaceuticals, where drugs, such as the combination of codeine and acetaminophen, interact to produce an enhanced painkilling effect. Another example might be a musical band. Individually, the band members each play a specific part of the music. Those singular parts may sound passable, but the real music only occurs when they are played harmoniously together. The band members become, in a sense, a synergistic team with a shared goal of creating a unified sound. The output is the magic of music.

Aristotle was writing about the physical world, but his concept is widely applied to management. If we think of synergistic teams as systems, we can see team members as components that work together in concert to process input and produce output. The system as a whole becomes more than the components put together, and the output is more than could be produced by the individual members working alone. Synergistic output is the goal when one is organizing a public relations team. The question, of course, is how to make synergy happen. There is no guaranteed formula for developing a cooperative team, but there are a few guidelines that can increase your chances for success. The first involves selection of team members.

Selecting Team Members

You most likely will be assigned to a public relations team. However, you occasionally may be in a position to assemble a team. In that case, your goal is to bring together people in such a way that results in both the strength that comes from diversity and the unity that comes from shared values.

One of the mistakes most of us tend to make is selecting people who are like ourselves, or selecting close friends as teammates. That can be a recipe for disaster. When putting a team together, it's a good idea to look for *diversity* in communication styles, skills, experiences, and resources, but strive for *similarity* in work ethics, goals, commitment, and availability.

Diversity Makes a Team Strong and Well-Rounded

It's the rare person who is truly skilled in everything that a public relations project requires. Some of us excel at writing, some have an eye for graphic design, some are good at math, some are great at research, some are stellar presenters, some are organizational or technological whizzes, and some have eagle-eye editorial skills—but few of us can do it all. Consider carefully your own skills. Are you good at writing, but perhaps a little shy in front of a group? Are you a terrific public speaker, but you have difficulty with spelling and grammar? Look for teammates who can fill in those gaps. Get started by listing all the skills you can identify that will be required for the project. A partial "wish list" might include the following skills and abilities:

- Budget development and cost estimates
- Desktop publishing
- Graphic arts and communication
- Logistics and scheduling
- Multimedia presentations
- Photography
- Record keeping or database management
- Quantitative and qualitative research methodologies
- Social media strategizing
- Web construction
- Writing and editing

Diverse Experiences. Beyond diverse skills, a diversity of experiences can strengthen your team. Consider each person's background. Who has done professional or volunteer work similar to the project you are planning? Who has traveled or has experiences different from your own to lend cultural insights to the team? Who has completed academic courses or professional seminars that pertain to the project? The more variety of experiential knowledge you can bring to your team, the stronger the team is likely to be.

Diverse Temperaments and Communication Styles. People do not always approach collaboration in the same way. Our differences can both strengthen a team and drive us crazy, so understanding those differences is essential. Some people tend to be direct, are goal oriented, and tend to drive others toward that goal. Others couch their words in ways that express support. They value a diversity of ideas, but are sometimes seen as indecisive in their efforts to be supportive. Still others may prefer to consider all aspects of a situation before expressing their thoughts. They are analytical and detail oriented, but are sometimes seen as aloof. Finally, some people prefer face-to-face conversation and are expressive—occasionally to the point of distraction. Each communication type has its own strengths and weaknesses, and each tends to lean toward a preferred communication channel. Expressive communicators, for example, might prefer face-to-face communication, while those who favor reflection and self-editing are more likely to use written forms of communication, such as e-mail.

Consider a team in which everyone is direct, decisive, and goal oriented. Collaborative decision making would be difficult, indeed, since each team member would be pushing for his or her own ideas and possibly ignoring those of others. Similarly, a team comprised solely of supportive communicators may have difficulty making decisions because the members are hesitant to discount their teammates' ideas. When forming a team, then, it's best to find potential teammates who have different communication styles or approaches to decision making than your own. Such instruments as the Myers-Briggs personality types (http://www.myersbriggs.org) or the Kiersey Temperament Sorter (KTS®-II) at http://www.kiersey.com are useful tools for this process.

Diverse Resources. Strong teams are made stronger when members bring a variety of resources to the table. Look for individuals with media contacts, relationships with vendors, appropriate computer hardware and software skills, raw materials, volunteer bases, and other resources that might be useful for the project.

Similarities Make a Team Cohesive and Functional

Similar Goals. Beyond diversity of skills and abilities, communication styles, experiences, and resources, synergistic teams are typically characterized by certain similarities among team members. The first, of course, is the shared goal or vision. Every member of the team must envision the same outcome and want to accomplish the same results. All team members should agree on the standard to be achieved. If even one person has a different goal or higher or lower standards than the rest of the team, the disparity is bound to reduce overall team effectiveness and can lead to serious internal ruptures.

Similar Work Ethics. Each team member should have a similar approach to work. Problems arise when some members are procrastinators and others are not; when some are punctual and others are chronically late; when some are intense workers and others are relaxed or even lazy. Strive for a team in which every member tackles work projects with similar energy, enthusiasm, and timeliness.

Similar Commitment Levels. Each member of a successful and synergistic team will have a similar level of commitment to the project. Look for team members who are willing and able to devote equivalent levels of time and effort to the group project. This is not to say that everyone must commit to a particular percentage of time or portion of the project. Rather, like work ethic, it is a level of effort to which team members are willing to commit for the project at hand.

Similar Schedules and Availability. Scheduling and availability are critical in all teamwork. No matter how good a team member's work ethic might be or how fully committed to the project the individual is, if the schedule is not viable, neither is participation on the team. Discern in advance meeting availability of all potential team members and look for those with schedules and time obligations that will allow for regular team meetings and efficient project scheduling.

Other Considerations for Building Synergistic Teams

Friendships. Keep in mind that a public relations team is a *business relationship*, not a *personal relationship*. Good friends can make poor teammates, for a variety of reasons. First, personal friends on a team can create uneven group dynamics, often splitting teams down the middle. Second, friends sometimes take advantage of the relationship or each other, expecting special favors or allowances that other team members would not get. In other words, a close personal relationship that is brought into a business-oriented team can jeopardize both the friendship and the team. Does this mean that if you have worked together before, you should avoid working together again in a team? Absolutely not! When former coworkers are involved in teams, they can actually contribute to higher group productivity (Parise & Rollag, 2010). The key is to keep interpersonal relationships on a professional level when working in teams.

Actions Speak Louder Than Words. Anyone can say anything about themselves. Make determinations about the people with whom you want to work based on what they have to show for themselves. Are they always on time and prepared? Do they conduct themselves professionally? Can they show you their work and accomplishments? Can they demonstrate the abilities and qualities they claim? Choose teammates carefully, based on performance rather than assertions. We have to live with the consequences of our choices. Poor group composition can seriously curtail team development, reducing or even destroying all productivity.

As you work through the public relations process, you may note that the relationships among team members and between the team and the client move through a series of stages. That is due, in part, to the fact that teams tend to evolve through a predictable life cycle.

The Life Cycles of Teams

Even with an ideal group of people, team members are likely to experience dissent and conflict in predictable stages. One of the earliest models of team development, which is still widely used today, is a four-stage process that Bruce Tuckman developed in 1965 on the basis of 50 empirical studies. Tuckman and Mary Ann Jensen (1977) later added a fifth stage, based on 22 additional studies. The resulting five stages are (1) Forming, (2) Storming, (3) Norming, (4) Performing, and (5) Adjourning.

1. *Forming*

   The first, *forming* stage of team development occurs as the new team members are selected and introduced to one another. During this phase, which is essentially a period of orientation, team members work independently. They exchange contact information and get acquainted, both with each other and with the team's goals and objectives. The team addresses such topics as the task at hand, general meeting times, preliminary division of labor, logistics, and other housekeeping issues. In this early stage, members' behaviors tend to be motivated by a desire for acceptance, so they typically avoid conflict as they gather and assess information about each other.

2. *Storming*

   The second, *storming* stage of team development occurs once team members' values, leadership styles, ideas, and perspectives begin to emerge. Some members may test the standards established during the forming stage. Here, the team also delves more deeply into the problem to be solved, and some members may respond emotionally to other team members or the requirements of the project. Of course, this can lead to confrontation and conflict as members attempt to resolve their differences. If members cannot reach mutually satisfactory resolutions during this stage, the team may become permanently dysfunctional. Although the storming phase can be unpleasant, it brings both interpersonal and goal-related issues to the fore and allows the team to develop. If all team members stay focused on productivity and professionalism, the team emerges from the storming phase strong, cohesive, and productive.

3. *Norming*

   The team reaches the third stage of development when members agree on the ultimate goal and a general plan for attaining it. All members become invested in achieving the goal and take responsibility for doing so, even at the expense of their personally held views. New team standards may evolve during this *norming* phase, and members' roles may converge or change. At this stage, the group begins to function as a productive team.

4. *Performing*

   High-functioning, synergistic teams reach the fourth stage of *performing* as a cohesive unit. At this point, team members can function interdependently, are knowledgeable about the project, and motivated to accomplish it. Team structures, norms, and standards are now well established, and members' energies are focused on achieving the team's goals, rather than on conflict resolution.

5. *Adjourning*

   The final stage of *adjourning* involves completion of the task or attainment of the team's goal. During this phase, members prepare to disengage from each other and from the project. Some may even go through a sense of loss or mourning as they anticipate dissolution of the team. Of course, only well-managed teams leave members nostalgic as they disperse.

Managing Public Relations Teams

During the forming stage of team development, the first order of business should be to establish *team standards*. If standards are not discussed and established from the start, normative behaviors become institutionalized. Those norms become team

TABLE 2-1: Tuckman and Jensen's Five-Stage Life Cycle of Teams.

	Group Structure The pattern of interpersonal relationships; the way members act and relate to one another	Task Activity The content of interaction as related to the task at hand
Forming: orientation, testing and dependence	Testing and dependence	Orientation to the task
Storming: resistance to group influence and task requirements	Intragroup conflict	Emotional response to task demands
Norming: openness to other group members	Ingroup feeling and cohesiveness develop; new standards evolve and new roles are adopted	Open exchange of relevant interpretations; intimate, personal opinions are expressed
Performing: constructive action	Roles become flexible and functional; structural issues have been resolved; structure can support task performance	Interpersonal structure becomes the tool of task activities; group energy is channeled into the task; solutions can emerge
Adjourning: disengagement	Anxiety about separation and termination; sadness; feelings toward leader and group members	Self-evaluation

standards, which, once formed, are difficult to change. For example, if the team does not agree on regular meeting times, it is all too easy to find justifications for not meeting. The team norm then becomes sporadic meetings or no meetings. Another, more insidious example involves punctuality. If a person arrives a half-hour late to the first meeting and the team does nothing about it, the team standard automatically becomes one of people showing up whenever they please. Clearly, this destroys team efficiency and fragments both the team's work and team cohesion. These sorts of things can lead to a devastating storming stage from which the team may never recover. The solution is to establish and enforce appropriate and effective standards from the beginning

Establishing Team Norms

Productive team standards vary widely from team to team, but it's wise to consider at least five general ideas. First, identify and use individual team members' strengths. Determine individual assignments as appropriate to each person's skills and abilities. For example, a weak writer may be exceptional at graphic design or at developing research protocols. Capitalize on those strengths and assign the writing to a different team member.

Second, establish regular team meeting times and places, both with the client and for the team alone. Ensure that all members put the meetings on their calendars so there is no misunderstanding about where and when the team will meet. It is easier to cancel a regular meeting than to schedule one that fits members' disparate schedules. If the team has a regular meeting place and time, members are better able to plan their work and schedule other activities.

Third, punctuality should be mandatory. Allowing members to show up to meetings late demonstrates a lack of respect for people's time, reduces team productivity, and damages overall team function.

Fourth, include *every* team member in *all* communications. Texting, individual e-mails, and other forms of private communication invariably lead to duplication of efforts, some team members being uninformed, and eventually, team fragmentation. Synergistic teams function interdependently, which means that all members are engaged in all aspects of the team processes.

Finally, always keep the purpose of team meetings in mind. They are professional business meetings and all personal matters should be left at the door. Make the team meetings as businesslike, efficient, and productive as possible.

Conducting Team Meetings

Team productivity can be enhanced by taking certain steps to run efficient meetings. First, prepare a written agenda and stick to it. Develop the agenda with a specific meeting purpose or goal in mind and with stated times for accomplishing specific tasks. An agenda that includes time allocations for each topic helps keep the meeting on track, reduces irrelevant discussions, and maximizes meeting efficiency. Second, write minutes for all team meetings. Minutes should include brief descriptions of agreed-on action items or tasks to be accomplished, along with due dates and the names of the individuals responsible for their completion. This practice supports healthy team standards and ensures both personal accountability and adherence to a reasonable timeline. Third, begin and end meetings on time. Clear goals and specific, dedicated blocks of time for meetings help members plan their work and meet team deadlines.

Managing Team Attitudes

In the early stages of team projects, teams typically meet with both successes and failures. Either can work to the team's advantage or disadvantage in the long run. Bandura's (2000) work indicates that early successes can bolster team confidence and improve productivity. However, there is also evidence that team confidence established in the early stages of development can have a negative effect (Goncalo, Polman, & Maslach, 2010). The bottom line is that team members are well advised to stay focused on the project and to avoid either overconfidence or demoralization based on early results of team efforts. Every endeavor, whether successful or not, is a learning experience that prepares team members for their next challenge.

Managing Team Conflict

As mentioned above, conflict is a natural part of teamwork. The trick is to move through the storming stage and into the norming stage and to manage conflicts as they arise. But what happens if things go really wrong? What do you do about a team member who just doesn't do the work? Occasionally, a problem arises where one team member fails to contribute effectively to the team project. If this happens in your group, you should make every effort to resolve the problem and document your efforts in writing. Recall that keeping meeting minutes, which include individual assignments and due dates, helps establish member accountability. Here are a few steps to use in resolving team conflict:

1. Try to work out the difficulty as a team, rather than as individuals. Hold a face-to-face meeting that emphasizes team goals and how to reach them.

2. If tensions are running high, set ground rules for the meeting. These rules might include:

   a. Agreeing to seek solutions

   b. No name calling

c. No interrupting

d. Clear and open communication about the issue

e. Listening to truly understand each other's point of view

3. Ask questions and get a clear picture of the problem before attempting to develop solutions. Does the nonperformer understand the task to be accomplished? Sometimes, an individual simply needs additional guidance and direction. Perhaps the team member has been assigned a task for which he or she is ill suited, which might indicate a redistribution of assignments. In fact, synergistic teams often allow team members to choose their own roles in the project.

4. Do not fall into the trap of casting blame. Approach the problem as a team issue and brainstorm possible resolutions. Stay calm and think of constructive, equitable options that meet all team members' needs.

5. Look for areas of negotiation and compromise.

6. Once through this process may not be enough. Counsel and discuss the situation with the underperforming individual at least three times.

7. Document all efforts to correct the problem. In a professional workplace, due process ensures that every effort has been made to help an individual become a contributing team member.

8. Seek outside counsel to help resolve the conflict. Sometimes, an objective view of the problem reveals fresh answers.

Obviously, not every team with which we work will be synergistic, but these steps mitigate problems. Recall, too, from our examination of communication models in Chapter 1 that inherent cultural, experiential, temperamental, or ideological differences can lead to misunderstandings among teammates and between a team and its client, but those differences also can strengthen the team. These phenomena are evident, as well, when generational differences (chronological, professional, or both) exist. One relatively little understood aspect of public relations is the interaction between new and seasoned practitioners.

On Mentoring and Being Mentored

Why should we think about mentorship in public relations? Well, consider that much of public relations practice is really mentorship to clients. We provide public relations counsel and advice, even as we develop

our own formal and informal mentorships in the workplace. Synergistic teams, in many ways, are self-mentoring groups. We therefore should think of ourselves as mentors to our teammates and seek mentorship from those with knowledge or skills that we may lack. This typically occurs when a seasoned practitioner mentors an entry-level person, but "reverse mentoring" also occurs in the workplace.

Professors Betsy Hays and Doug Swanson are looking into the phenomenon of reverse mentoring, which is becoming more common as young, technologically-savvy practitioners enter the workforce. Hays and Swanson (2011), citing Kenneth Pyle, note that:

Reverse mentoring involves a structured workplace relationship between senior staff members and younger/less experienced workers. Typically, the younger workers have less expertise within the organization but more technological familiarity and skills. The pairing of senior staff with more technologically knowledgeable workers brings about the education of "older folks who can't figure out technology."

(Pyle, 2005, p. 40)

According to Hays and Swanson, one implication of reverse mentoring is that different generations of workers bring different values, attitudes, and psychological constructs to the table, which leads to frustration and loss of value. Therefore, just as older practitioners need preparation to understand young coworkers, new practitioners need preparation to establish reverse mentorships with older coworkers. In PR terms, we need to understand our audiences to communicate effectively and build positive relationships with them.

Tying It All Together

Effective team management enables public relations practitioners to accomplish far more than is possible as individuals. Because public relations is so broad and encompasses expertise in many disparate areas, it is often practiced through teams, and team members can and do learn from each other.

This chapter drew distinctions between groups and teams, and stressed the desirability of developing synergistic teams for the practice of public relations. It outlined various characteristics to consider in potential teammates that would maximize the possibility of forming a high-performance team. Members of high-performance teams typically share similar goals, commitment, work ethic, and schedules, but bring to the table diverse skills and abilities, experiences, communication styles, and resources.

Teams typically move through four stages of development, including a period of storming or conflict, and then into a final, fifth stage of adjournment. Synergistic teams move through the storming stage to reach operational working relationships that accomplish the shared goals. They establish appropriate team norms, conduct efficient meetings, manage conflict, and maintain team standards throughout the life of the project.

Name _____Date _____

REFLECT AND REVIEW

1. Think about groups of people that you observe on a daily basis. Are they teams or groups? In the table below, briefly describe your observations of one "team" and one "group."

Characteristics	My Team	My Group
Name (task or project):		
Similar or diverse? • Goals • Work ethics • Commitment level • Schedule		
Similar or diverse? • Communication styles • Skills • Experiences • Resources		

2. In the table below, fill in the characteristics of each stage of group development.

TABLE 2-1: Tuckerman and Jensen's Five-Stage Life Cycle of Teams.

	Group Structure The pattern of interpersonal relationships; the way members act and relate to one another	Task Activity The content of interaction as related to the task at hand
Forming		
Storming		
Norming		
Performing		
Adjourning		

3. Take the Communication Style Inventory below and discuss the results with your teammates.

    a. What is your personal communication style?

        _____

    b. What annoys you about each of the other styles?

        _____

        _____

        _____

        _____

    c. What do you value about each of the other styles?

        _____

        _____

        _____

        _____

    d. Do you have a diversity of communication styles on your team?

        _____

    e. How do you think your team will function if you all have similar communication styles?

        i. Supporter/Relater?

            _____

            _____

        ii. Analyzer/Thinker?

            _____

            _____

iii. Promoter/Socializer?

_____

_____

iv. Controller/Director?

_____

_____

COMMUNICATION STYLE INVENTORY
(ALESSANDRA & O'CONNOR, 1996)

This is an informal instrument to help you identify your preferred communication style. Bear in mind that we typically use a variety of communication styles throughout any given day. There is no "right" or "wrong" style—only differences.

Instructions: For each of the items below, circle either A or B, whichever you believe most closely describes you in everyday situations.

1. A) I'm usually open to getting to know people personally and establishing relationships with them.

    B) I'm not usually open to getting to know people personally and establishing relationships with them.

2. A) I usually react slowly and deliberately.

    B) I usually react quickly and spontaneously.

3. A) I'm usually guarded about other people's use of my time.

    B) I'm usually open to other people's use of my time.

4. A) I usually introduce myself at social gatherings.

    B) I usually wait for others to introduce themselves to me at social gatherings.

5. A) I usually focus my conversations on the interests of the people involved, even if that means straying from the business or subject at hand.

    B) I usually focus my conversations on the tasks, issues, business, or subject at hand.

6. A) I'm usually not assertive, and I can be patient with a slow pace.

    B) I'm usually assertive, and at times I can be impatient with a slow pace.

7. A) I usually make decisions based on facts or evidence.

    B) I usually make decisions based on feelings, experiences, or relationships.

8. A) I usually contribute frequently to group conversations.

    B) I usually contribute infrequently to group conversations.

9. A) I usually prefer to work with and through others, providing support when possible.

    B) I usually prefer to work independently or dictate the conditions in terms of how others are involved.

10. A) I usually ask questions or speak tentatively and indirectly.

    B) I usually make empathic statements or directly express opinions.

11. A) I usually focus primarily on ideas, concepts, or results.

    B) I usually focus primarily on persons, interactions, and feelings.

12. A) I usually use gestures, facial expressions, and voice intonations to emphasize points.

    B) I usually do not use gestures, facial expressions, and voice intonations to emphasize points.

13. A) I usually accept others' points of view (ideas, feelings, and concerns).

    B) I usually don't accept others' points of view (ideas, feelings, and concerns).

14. A) I usually respond to risk and change in a cautious or predictable manner.

    B) I usually respond to risk and change in dynamic or unpredictable manner.

15. A) I usually prefer to keep personal feelings and thoughts private, sharing only when I wish to do so.

    B) I usually find it natural and easy to share and discuss my feelings with others.

16. A) I usually seek out new or different experiences and situations.

    B) I usually choose known or similar situations and relationships.

17. A) I'm usually responsive to others' agendas, interests, and concerns.

    B) I'm usually directed toward my own agendas, interests, and concerns.

18. A) I usually respond to conflict slowly and indirectly.

    B) I usually respond to conflict quickly and directly.

COMMUNICATION STYLES ANSWER SHEET

O	G	D	I
1A	1B	2B	2A
3B	3A	4A	4B
5A	5B	6B	6A
7B	7A	8A	8B
9A	9B	10B	10A
11B	11A	12A	12B
13A	13B	14B	14A
15B	15A	16A	16B
17A	17B	18B	18A

Total the numbers of items you circled in each column:

_____	_____	_____	_____
O	**G**	**D**	**I**

Circle O or G, whichever has the higher number.
Circle D or I, whichever has the higher number.

What It All Means:

If you circled the G and D, your communication style is that of a Controller/Director.
If you circled the O and D, your communication style is that of a Promoter/Socializer.
If you circled the O and I, your communication style is that of a Supporter/Relater.
If you circled the G and I, your communication style is that of an Analyzer/Thinker.

General Characteristics Of The Four Communication Styles

Supporter/Relater

- Harmonizer
- Values acceptance and stability in circumstances
- Slow with big decisions; dislikes change
- Builds networks of friends to help do work
- Good listener; timid about voicing contrary opinions; concerned for others' feelings
- Easy-going; likes slow, steady pace

- Friendly and sensitive; no person is unlovable
- Relationship oriented

Analyzer/Thinker

- Assessor
- Values accuracy in details and being right
- Plans thoroughly before deciding to act
- Prefers to work alone
- Introverted; quick to think and slow to speak; closed about personal matters
- Highly organized; even plans spontaneity!
- Cautious, logical, thrifty approach
- Thoughtful; no problem is too big to ponder
- Idea oriented

Promoter/Socializer

- Entertainer
- Values enjoyment and helping others with the same
- Full of ideas and impulsive in trying them
- Wants to work to be fun for everyone
- Talkative and open about self; asks others' opinions; loves to brainstorm
- Flexible; easily bored with routine
- Intuitive, creative, spontaneous, flamboyant approach
- Optimist; nothing is beyond hope
- Celebration oriented

Controller/Director

- Commander
- Values getting the job done
- Decisive risk taker
- Good at delegating work to others
- Not shy, but private about personal matters; comes on strong in conversation
- Likes to be where the action is
- Take charge, enterprising, competitive, efficient approach
- Fearless; no obstacle is too big to tackle
- Results oriented

CHAPTER 2 REFERENCES AND RESOURCES

Alessandra, T., & O'Connor, M. J. (1996). *The platinum rule.* New York: Warner Brooks.

Aristotle. (c. 335–323 BCE). *The metaphysics* (Book VIII, Part 6). New York: Cosimo.

Aristotle, & Freese, J. (1959). *The "Art" of Rhetoric.* Cambridge, Mass.: Harvard University Press

Bandura, A. (2000). Exercise of human agency through collective-efficacy. *Current Directions in Psychological Science, 9*(3), 75–78.

Devine, D. J., & Clayton, L. D. (1999). Teams in organizations. *Small Group Research, 30*(6), 678–712.

Goncalo, J., Polman, E., & Maslach, C. (2010). Can confidence come too soon? Collective efficacy, conflict and group performance over time. *Organizational Behavior & Human Decision Processes, 113*(1), 13–24.

Hays, B. A., & Swanson, D. J. (2011). Prevalence and success of reverse mentoring in public relations. *Public Relations Journal, 5*(4), 1–18.

Katzenbach, J. R., & Smith, D. K. (1993). The discipline of teams. *Harvard Business Review, 71*(March–April), 111–146.

Parise, S., & Rollag, K. (2010). Emergent network structure and initial group performance: The moderating role of pre-existing relationships. *Journal of Organizational Behavior, 31*(6), 877–897.

Pyle, K. (2005). Youth are the present. *Telephony, 246,* 40. (Cited in Hays, B. A., & Swanson, D. J. (2011). Prevalence and success of reverse mentoring in public relations. *Public Relations Journal, 5*(4), 17)

Thomas, B. (1998, September 9). Babe Ruth quotation in *Congressional Record,* V. 144, Pt. 14, September 9, 1998 to September 21, 1998, p. 19813.

Tuckman, B. W. (1965). Developmental sequence in small groups. *Psychological Bulletin, 63,* 384–399. (Reprinted in *Group Facilitation: A Research and Applications Journal, 3,* 66–81. Retrieved from ABI/INFORM Global [Document ID: 353167091]).

Tuckman, B. W., & Jensen, M. A. (1977). Stages of small-group development revisited. *Group & Organization Studies, 2*(4), 419–427.

Chapter 3
Preparing and Proposing a Public Relations Plan

Our goals can only be reached through a vehicle of a plan, in which we must fervently believe, and upon which we must vigorously act. There is no other route to success.

~ Pablo Picasso

This chapter outlines the general structure of a PR plan and contextualizes it within the four-step public relations process. It provides suggestions for incorporating a plan into a formal proposal of work and provides information on writing a letter of transmittal and an executive summary.

LEARNING OBJECTIVES:

The information presented in this chapter will enable you to:

1. Develop a cohesive structure for a public relations plan.

2. Systematically develop a public relations plan, using the four-step process.

3. Incorporate a written public relations plan into a formal proposal.

4. Write an executive summary of a public relations proposal.

5. Write a letter of transmittal to accompany the proposal.

Whether you're working for a corporation, a nonprofit organization, a government, an educational institution, or a public relations firm, you need to be able to develop detailed plans for your public relations programs. You have to come to some agreement with your supervisor or client about the nature and scope of the work you will do, how much it will cost, how long it will take, what tools will be used, and what your program will accomplish. This chapter addresses the specific components of a public relations plan and then describes how that plan might be incorporated into a formal work proposal. The chapter also addresses writing a formal letter of transmittal for a proposal.

Structuring the Public Relations Plan

A well-written public relations plan serves multiple purposes. First, of course, it outlines what you plan to do, why you plan to do it, and what outcomes you want to

FIGURE 3-1
A public relations team must do careful research and analysis to identify target publics and develop appropriate strategies, tactics, and tools with which to reach those publics.

achieve, as well as how you will measure those outcomes. Second, the plan explains to the client the general scope of the work you propose to do, how long it will take, and how much the client can expect to spend if the plan is accepted. Third, a plan provides the practitioner with a roadmap for implementation. It describes, step by step, the objectives to be met, the messages to be sent, the audiences to be reached, the most appropriate strategies and tools with which to reach them, the target dates for each step, how much can be spent, and how to measure success.

Specific formats and structures for PR plans vary widely, but the following outline shows the major components that should be included and is organized according to the four-step public relations process of Research, Planning, Implementation, and Evaluation.

A. Research

   1. Situation Analysis

      a. Political, Economic, Social, and Technological issues faced by the client (PEST analysis).

      b. Client Strengths, Weaknesses, Opportunities, and Threats (SWOT analysis)

      c. Problem Statement

   2. Analysis of Key Publics

      a. Demographics

      b. Psychographics

      c. Influencers and Self Interests

      d. Relationships to the Client

B. Planning

    1. Goals and Objectives

    2. Key Messages for Each Key Public

        a. Primary Publics

        b. Secondary Publics

C. Implementation

    1. Strategies to Reach Each Key Public

    2. Tools and Tactics to Be Used

    3. Calendar

    4. Budget

D. Evaluation

    1. Evaluation Criteria

    2. Evaluation Tools and Measurements

    3. Anticipated Results

The outline shown here represents only the skeleton of a full public relations plan. Like a physical skeleton, the individual bones must be tied together in some way. Just as biological skeletons are held together with connective tendons, ligaments, and muscles, a well-written plan is held together with grammatically correct, complete sentences, internal summaries, and transitions from paragraph to paragraph and section to section. Remember, you are writing a public relations plan, not constructing an outline. The sections are not simply discrete, fill-in-the-blank holes. They build on one another, and the writing should reflect that.

Just as biological skeletons are held together with connective tendons, ligaments, and muscles, a well-written plan is held together with grammatically correct, complete sentences, internal summaries, and transitions.

We examine in detail each major section of the plan in Chapters 5, 6, 7, and 8. For now, let's briefly consider the general purpose of each section. Keep in mind that *every tool, every decision must be supported by research and analysis and justified* in your PR plan. Most of that justification stems from the first section of the plan.

Research

The first section of any public relations plan provides you with the background you need to make informed decisions on how to proceed and lets the client know you have done your homework. Here, you are demonstrating to the client two things: (1) that you understand the client's organizational situation, both in terms of the environmental factors that affect it and in terms of its internal strengths and weaknesses, and (2) that you have identified appropriate publics to reach and analyzed the nature of those publics. The Research section of the PR plan both identifies the resources that are used to gather information and describes the specific information drawn from those resources. In other words, you are stating not only what you know, but also how you know it.

The Situation Analysis. A thorough situation analysis investigates the client's Political, Economic, Social, and Technological (PEST) influences as well as Strengths, Weaknesses, Opportunities, and Threats (SWOT). A PEST analysis can inform the SWOT, so it's wise to do both.

As shown in Figure 3-2, the PEST analysis looks at four key environmental factors that affect social systems at local, national, and global levels:

- *Political* factors, such as taxes, laws (labor laws, environmental impact laws, trade laws, etc.), government regulations, and zoning issues.

- *Economics* includes currency exchange rates, interest rates, inflation, and economic growth or recession.

- *Social* issues address such things as cultural influences and trending attitudes and interests.

- *Technological* considerations include research and development of new technologies and the rate of technological change.

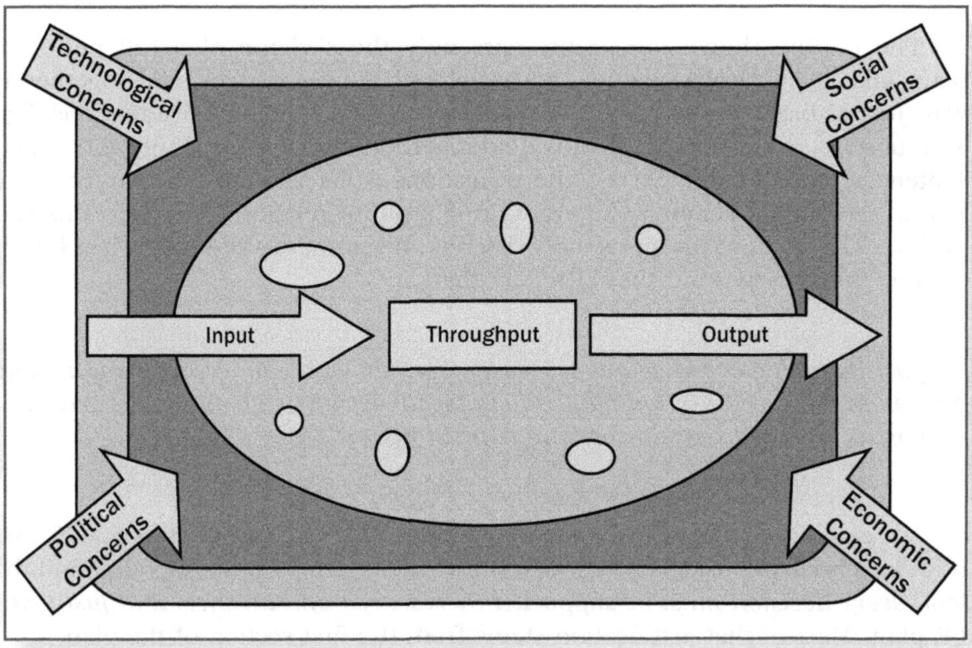

FIGURE 3-2
Political, Economic, Social, and Technological factors in the environment affect all social systems. (Figure adapted from Athey, 1982.)

Understanding environmental factors establishes the opportunities and threats in a SWOT analysis. Here, we analyze factors that are both internal and external to the organization. One way to do this is to develop a grid, such as the one shown in Figure 3-3, listing the following research-based factors:

- *Strengths* are internal to the organization and characteristic of it. For example, a strength in a nonprofit organization might be its volunteer base (either in terms of numbers or enthusiasm or both).

- *Weaknesses* are also internal to the organization and characteristic of it. For example, low employee morale might be a weakness, particularly in times of economic downturn and potential layoffs.

- *Opportunities* are external to the organization and present positive prospects for action.

- *Threats* are external to the organization and present hazards or dangers that may disrupt or minimize the social system.

Bear in mind that both the PEST and SWOT are the basis of *analysis*, not simply checklists. Once you have identified the critical external and internal factors that affect organizational health, you need to explain how they do so. This means writing a paragraph or two that synthesizes and analyzes all the information.

The Problem Statement. The situation analysis provides the foundation for the problem statement. The problem statement is a one- or two-sentence declaration of the problem the PR plan is being developed to solve *or* the opportunity on which the plan will build.

Writing the situation analysis can be tricky, especially when describing a client's weaknesses. You need to be honest about flaws that your research reveals and address them in a way that does not insult the client. Make sure you do thorough research to support your claims. This may involve primary research, as well as secondary research, both of which are addressed in Chapter 5.

The Audience Analysis. Beyond the situation analysis, the Research section of the PR plan identifies and describes the characteristics of the key publics to be reached. This information requires extensive research into your primary, secondary, and tertiary target publics. You need to know three critical things: (1) who the target publics are, based on the problem statement you have established (there probably will be other publics that you will not address for the project at hand), (2) what interests and motivates these people, and (3) the channels through which they get their information.

FIGURE 3-3 Beyond developing a basis for the problem statement, a SWOT analysis identifies potential risks and benefits of future actions. Strengths and weaknesses are internal to the organization. Opportunities and threats are part of the organization's environment.

Understanding the values, attitudes, lifestyles, and motivations of the target publics is essential for developing effective messages and strategies and for selecting the appropriate tools with which to reach them. Without this information, you are doomed to miscommunicating with your target publics or, worse yet, mistargeting them altogether.

Planning

As noted above, to write effective messages, you must have a clear understanding of the values, attitudes, lifestyles, and motivations of the targeted publics, which are drawn from the Research section. Once the client's key problem or opportunity is identified and appropriate publics are targeted, you are ready to begin planning the

FIGURE 3-4 The situation analysis and problem identification forms the basis for a sound strategy, which in turn, unifies and guides the implementation of a public relations plan. Measurable objectives help develop appropriate evaluation methods. Evaluation, in turn, becomes the basis of research for a subsequent program.

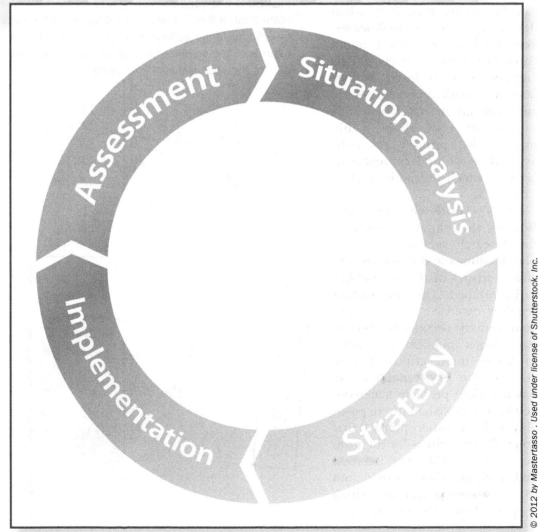

public relations program. This section of the PR plan, which Chapter 6 explains in detail, outlines the client's goal(s) and establishes the measurable results you plan to accomplish, which will help the client achieve those goals. The Planning section also describes the key messages the targeted publics should receive to reach your stated objectives. This, then, establishes the basis for determining which strategies, tools, and tactics will best deliver your key messages to the targeted publics.

Implementation

The Implementation section of your PR plan, which is fully addressed in Chapter 7, describes in detail the strategies, tools, and tactics you plan to use to effectively deliver key messages to target publics. Once again, it is not a discrete, stand-alone section; it provides ideas that are built on the information and analyses of your research and planning, and it must justify each of those ideas.

This section of your plan explains the general approaches you believe will best appeal to the targeted publics and why you selected them. It then outlines the tools and tactics you have selected to most effectively deliver your key messages to the target publics. This section also includes a detailed calendar, preferably in the form of a Gantt chart, and an itemized budget, which includes anticipated costs for every component of the proposed plan.

Sometimes, novice practitioners get so focused on getting all the components of the plan in order that they forget the creative side of the profession. This is a huge mistake. Be sure to include in this section the strategic "twist" that will establish your plan as fresh and creative, as well as the rationale behind your choices. Such things as creative tag lines, campaign identifications, mascots, and visual identifiers will elevate your plan from ordinary to exciting.

The Implementation section of your PR plan should not just be a laundry list of public relations tools and tactics. It should be a thorough description of how and when those tools and tactics will be implemented and why they were chosen over other possibilities. Consider this section the "assembly instructions" for your plan. Thus far, the plan has listed all the "parts" (strategies, tactics, messages, publics, etc.), and here, you explain how those parts must be put together to create a cohesive, functional whole. Once that is done, you are ready to describe how you will measure the success of the program.

Evaluation

Typically, organizational decision makers are interested primarily in the Return on Investment (ROI) of any undertaking, and that includes public relations programs. It's therefore critical that a PR plan include solid evaluation techniques. These stem from well-written and specific goals and objectives that appear in the Planning section of the plan. The program objectives, if written to incorporate measurability, establish the criteria for determining your success.

The Evaluation section of the PR plan revisits each objective in terms of how you plan to measure the extent to which it was accomplished. This section also describes the specific methods you will use to take those measurements. Will you count press clippings? Will you track visits to a website? What specific measurement tools will you use? You will need empirical evidence of your success, once the program has been implemented. This is the public relations equivalent of a carpenter measuring the space for building a cabinet.

Just "eyeballing" a space is not enough. A carpenter must use a tape measure to determine the exact dimensions of the cabinet (do the research and set the objective), measure all the components and build it (implement the plan), and then measure the finished cabinet to verify that it will fit (evaluate the outcomes). The criterion is fitting the cabinet to the designated space. The measurement tool is the measuring tape. Similarly, your PR plan must spell out both your criteria for success and the measurement tools you will use to determine that success. See Chapter 8 for more information on public relations measurement tools.

Like our carpenter, it might be necessary to take some baseline measurements before a plan is implemented. Increasing awareness of a client's organization or product or service, for example, which is often a PR program goal, is typically measured with a preprogram survey of the target publics. This establishes a baseline of how many people are aware of the client. Once the PR program has been completed, a post-program survey will reveal the extent to which awareness has been raised as a result of your public relations program. At the very least, your plan must spell out the tools and methods you will use to evaluate the extent to which your objectives are met after the program is implemented. All of this means that a solid foundation in research methods and consideration of those methods as you write your goals and objectives allows you to demonstrate your plan's ROI, once it is implemented and complete.

Incorporating the Public Relations Plan into a Formal Work Proposal

It is not unusual for organizations to send *Requests for Proposals* (RFPs) to public relations firms. An RFP spells out what is to be accomplished through public relations and includes deadlines by which written responses must be submitted. The written response to an RFP is a *proposal* of work. An RFP may or may not include budgetary limits or timeframes, specific goals to be accomplished, information on key publics, and other important material. It is therefore critical that you read an RFP carefully and respond to each item in your proposal.

A proposal is a persuasive document. Its purpose is to *propose* your public relations plan to a potential client, as well as to *persuade* the client that your PR team is the best choice to provide the service. You may be competing with other PR firms for a job, and the written document probably will be the only basis on which the client decides whether to invite you to present your plan in person. Therefore, just as you would dress professionally for a job interview, it is critical that you prepare a professional, readable, and eye-catching written proposal.

Proposal formats vary widely, and some nice templates are available online through such websites as Microsoft Office and Apple support. In general, however, for professionalism and readability, the document should, at a minimum, have the following characteristics:

- A cover that indicates the public relations team name and contact information, the campaign identifier, and other information as appropriate

- A table of contents

- Consistent margins and adequate white space

- Descriptive headings and subheadings

- Numbered pages and clearly labeled sections

- Clearly labeled graphics, tables, and charts, as appropriate

- Computer-generated or typed index tabs for lengthy proposals

- Cohesive appearance throughout

- Binding (usually a comb or spiral binding) to hold the elements together

- Timely submission by the deadline

With a focus on professionalism, keep in mind as well, some things the printed proposal *must not* have:

- Grammatical, spelling, syntax, or typographical errors

- Smudges or wrinkled pages

- Low print quality

- Inconsistent use of fonts or graphics

credit line t/k

- Low-resolution or distorted graphics, especially of the client's logo

- Writing lifted directly from the client's materials (no client will pay for their own work!)

- Words, phrases, or ideas of others unless appropriately attributed

- Handwritten labels, tags, page numbers, or other components

- Loose pages or inserts

In addition to the proposal, you need to prepare a one- to two-page executive summary that provides the client with a "bird's-eye view" of the entire public relations plan and a one-page letter of transmittal. Both of these items are described later in this chapter. Two versions of a full sample proposal, prepared by Morgan Marketing and Public Relations, LLC for Golden Island Gourmet Snacks, also appear in Appendices 8 and 9.

Like their formats, proposal structures can vary, but a written public relations proposal typically includes the information outlined below. Note that in this outline, Sections II and III constitute the **public relations plan**, the elements of which are emphasized in **bold italics**:

I. Introduction

    A. Brief background of the client organization

    B. Description of who is offering the proposal and why

    C. Overview of the problems and potential solutions

    D. Rationale for public relations as a cost-effective approach to the problem

II. Problem Statement

    A. ***Research***

        1. ***Situation Analysis***

           a. ***Political, Economic, Social, and Technological issues faced by the client (PEST Analysis)***

           b. ***Client Strengths, Weaknesses, Opportunities, and Threats (SWOT Analysis)***

           c. ***Problem Statement***

        2. ***Analysis of Key Publics***

           a. ***Demographics***

           b. ***Psychographics***

           c. ***Influencers and Self Interests***

           d. ***Relationships to the Client***

III. Work Statement

    A. ***Planning***

        1. ***Goals and Objectives***

        2. ***Key Messages for Each Key Public***

           a. ***Primary Publics***

           b. ***Secondary Publics***

    B. ***Implementation***

        1. ***Strategies to Reach Each Key Public***

        2. ***Tools and Tactics to Be Used***

        3. ***Calendar***

        4. ***Budget***

    C. ***Evaluation***

        1. ***Evaluation Criteria***

        2. ***Evaluation Tools and Measurements***

        3. ***Anticipated Results***

IV. Qualifications

    A. Public relations team members' individual duties and backgrounds

    B. Reporting procedures

V. Appendix

    A. Samples of all proposed products (brochures, newsletters, websites, news releases, etc.)

B. Media lists and other working documents

C. *NOTE: Students should include an alphabetized, detailed list of references that you used for your research (APA or MLA style)*

As you can see, Sections II and III of the proposal are simply the public relations plan, which was addressed earlier in this chapter. The new components that surround the plan are Sections I, IV, and V: the Introduction, the Qualifications, and the Appendix. Let's look at each of these new sections.

Proposal Section I: Introduction

The introduction to a proposal establishes the reader's expectations for what will be included in the body of the proposal. It should accomplish three things: (1) demonstrate to the client that you have "done your homework" and understand the nature of the organization, (2) orient the reader to your team and to public relations (as opposed to advertising) as an appropriate solution to the stated problem, and (3) provide a preview of the proposed public relations plan.

The proposal introduction need not be lengthy, but it should provide the reader with an orientation to the rest of the document. The introduction includes a brief background of the client organization. Remember, you are directly addressing the client in this document, so the background information is not news to them. You simply want to incorporate a few sentences that demonstrate your own understanding of the client and its current status. Similarly, you should include a few introductory remarks about your public relations team, referring to the RFP, if there is one, and why you are submitting the proposal. This section also provides a brief overview of the stated problem or problems, what will occur if the problem is not resolved, and outlines some potential solutions. If you are not responding to a public relations RFP, include a rationale for why a public relations program is a cost effective approach to the problem. Again, the introduction is brief, and should not exceed one or two pages. You want to get the client to the meat of your PR plan as quickly as possible, which are Sections II and III, the Problem Statement and the Work Statement.

Remember that the proposal is a persuasive document; its purpose is to "sell" your public relations plan to the client. Beyond the strength of the public relations plan, your qualifications and examples of your deliverables must persuade the client that not only is the proposed plan desirable, but that your team is qualified to deliver the campaign.

Proposal Section IV: Qualifications

When outlining the public relations team's qualifications, you are trying to demonstrate that your team members have both the individual depth and the collective breadth of experience to effectively implement and evaluate the plan you are proposing. You also want to inform the client of how you will communicate throughout the program.

Some firms keep a file of individual biographical sheets for each employee that can be quickly inserted into proposals. Such bios should include each person's experience, skills, abilities, special interests, and other information that demonstrates both motivation and competency to provide the specific services outlined in the PR plan. The goal is to offer the client a well-rounded team that is ready, willing, and very able to attain the stated goals.

Proposal Section V: Appendix

The proposal appendix includes a variety of support materials, including samples of all deliverables proposed in the work statement. For example, if you are proposing to produce and distribute a variety of collateral materials such as brochures, flyers, door hangers, and calendars, the appendix should contain mock-ups of each of those items. Similarly, the appendix contains speech outlines, descriptions and layouts of news releases, and working documents such as media lists. Like the rest of the proposal, each item must be pristine, original, and free of errors. Media lists should be complete and up-to-date, with accurate contact information for each editor, journalist, producer, or programmer.

Typically, the text of the proposal includes small tables and charts to help the reader understand key points. For example, the budget in the implementation section of the work statement might include a small pie chart within the text to illustrate general distribution of funds. A more detailed itemization can go in the appendix. The trick is to be sure that all embedded tables and charts are only *illustrations* that clarify the information you are writing in narrative form. They cannot stand alone to convey the information. In addition, the proposal should be submitted with two additional documents: a letter of transmittal and an executive summary.

Additional Proposal Materials: Letter of Transmittal and Executive Summary

The letter of transmittal and executive summary are not part of a formal proposal document, but they should be included as part of the proposal package. Both items play a role in presenting a complete and coherent proposal. They are presented last here, because they are best written after you have completed the proposal or plan. Remember, it's much easier (and more accurate) to summarize something *after* you have written it than it is before you have written it.

The Letter of Transmittal

The first document that accompanies a public relations plan or proposal is the letter of transmittal, which constitutes the formal transmission of the proposal to the client. Take a moment to reflect on the communication models presented in Chapter 1. Remember that the sender (encoder/decoder) must transmit a message to a receiver (decoder/encoder). Now consider your PR team as the sender and the client as the receiver. The information in the written proposal is your message, and it must be transmitted to the client. That is the purpose of the letter of transmittal.

Check, recheck, and check again for spelling and accuracy, particularly of names, titles, addresses, and phone numbers.

The letter of transmittal precedes the written proposal and describes the general nature of your public relations plan. Your letter should be no more than one page. If your public relations plan is being sent to a decision maker within your own organization, it should be written in memorandum form. If it is being sent to an external potential client, the format is that of a formal letter on company letterhead. A suggested general structure of the transmittal letter, based on a list by Craig Miyamoto, APR (n.d.) is as follows:

XYZ Public Relations

123 Cinnamon Boulevard
Spice City, CA 12345
Phone: 123-456-7890 Fax: 123-456-0987
E-Mail: herb@xyz.com
Web: www.xyz.com

January 1, 2012

John Jones
ABCD Corporation
8910 Yucca Bean Avenue
Spice City, CA 12345

Dear Mr. Jones:

In response to your Request for Proposals of December 12, it is a pleasure to submit the enclosed proposal for a public relations campaign to increase awareness of your innovative door lock.

As you'll note in the executive summary, the proposed campaign partners with community-based nonprofit organizations and local law enforcement agencies to encourage home security and safety. We anticipate completion of the program by the end of the year and project a 10% increase in sales of the lock by that time.

We will be happy to arrange an in-person presentation of the plan at your convenience, in our offices or in yours. In the meantime, please feel free to contact us if you have any questions.

Thank you for the opportunity of presenting our ideas to you. We believe our proposal will meet and exceed your needs, and we look forward to working with you.

Sincerely,

Herb Carraway
Account Executive
XYZ Public Relations

FIGURE 3-5 Example of a letter of transmittal.

1. A cordial first paragraph that states you are submitting the enclosed proposal. If the proposal has been prepared in response to an RFP, mention that here.
2. A reference to the executive summary.
3. A brief description of the plan and its anticipated outcomes, including the ROI. Summarize anticipated expenses, income, and net profit or loss. This is essential, because a client usually is most interested in knowing the "bottom line."
4. An optimistic statement that you look forward to presenting the plan or discussing it further in person.
5. A closing paragraph that thanks the client for the opportunity to submit the proposal.

Check, recheck, and check again for spelling and accuracy, particularly of names, titles, addresses, and phone numbers. Misspelling a client's name (even by misplacing an apostrophe) can cost you your job—and such errors will leap off the page at the client.

The Executive Summary

The second document that accompanies a public relations plan or proposal is the executive summary, which usually appears as the first pages in the bound document. Decision makers often cannot or do not take the time to read a plan thoroughly until they have determined that it is worth serious consideration. The purpose of the executive summary is to describe the fundamental facts of your plan and entice the reader to read the entire document. It should be no more than two pages long and include the following essential information:

1. The problem statement, along with a brief rationale for it

2. Program goal: your solution to the identified problem

3. An overview of targeted publics

4. A summary of the plan's goals and objectives

5. The plan's overarching strategy and key tactics to be used

6. Recommended budget: Summarize anticipated expenses, income, and net profit or loss

7. An estimate of how long the proposed program will take and when it will conclude

8. Evaluation methods: how you will measure the extent to which you will have achieved your stated objectives

Clearly, with only two pages for the summary, economy of words is crucial. Be sure to think about how those words appear on the page. As with all public relations writing, your goal is readability, as well as communicating the information, so the layout should incorporate adequate margins, readable fonts, and a clear organization.

Tying It All Together

A public relations plan is designed to help decision makers determine an optimal course of action and to guide the team responsible for implementation and evaluation. The plan describes (1) a client's situation, (2) a key problem to solve *or* an opportunity on which to build, (3) the organizational and public relations goals and objectives, (4) the key audiences to be reached, (5) the strategies, tactics, and tools that best reach those audiences, (6) how the tools and tactics will be implemented, (7) projected costs and timeline, (8) how the outcomes will be measured, and (9) the anticipated results.

A proposal for work is a persuasive document that contains a full public relations plan, as well as information that demonstrates a team's ability to carry out the plan. It is typically prepared in response to a Request for Proposal (RFP) and submitted with a letter of transmittal and an executive summary.

REFLECT AND REVIEW

1. What are the five sections of a public relations proposal?

   1. _Intro_____
   2. _Problem Statement_____
   3. _Work Statement_____
   4. _Qualifications_____
   5. _Apendex_____

2. Which part of a public relations plan contains the goals and objectives?

   1. Research

   (2.) Planning

   3. Implementation

   4. Evaluation

3. What is the purpose of the executive summary?

   Overview of plan. get client to want
   _to read proposal._____

4. Which part of a public relations proposal outlines the duties, motivations, skills, and abilities of the public relations team?

   1. Introduction

   2. Problem statement

   3. Work statement

   4. Evaluation

   5. Qualifications

5. Which part of a public relations proposal contains the situation analysis?

   1. Introduction

   2. Problem statement

   3. Work statement

   4. Qualifications

   5. Appendix

CHAPTER 3 REFERENCES AND RESOURCES

Athey, T. H. (1982). *Systematic systems approach: An integrated method for solving systems problems.* Englewood Cliffs, NJ: Prentice-Hall.

Miyamoto, C. T. (n.d.). *How to write a comprehensive public relations plan.* Retrieved from http://www.hotwireprc.com/documents/How%20To%20Write%20A%20Comprehensive%20Public%20Relations%20Plan.pdf

Picasso, P. (n.d.). BrainyQuote.com. Retrieved from http://www.brainyquote.com/quotes/authors/p/pablo_picasso_3.html

Chapter 4
Build It, but Will They Come? Persuasion, Creativity, and Newsworthiness

Think left and think right and think low and think high. Oh, the thinks you can think up if only you try!

~Dr. Seuss

This chapter discusses the importance of originality and creativity in developing effective, persuasive messages. It also addresses newsworthiness and creative angles for pitches.

LEARNING OBJECTIVES

The information presented in this chapter will enable you to:

1. Describe Petty and Cacioppo's Elaboration Likelihood Model of persuasion.

2. Use Grunig's situational theory to identify active and passive audiences.

3. Develop the "Big Idea" that will set your program apart.

4. Establish persuasive strategies that appeal to various target publics.

5. Develop an "angle" for your program that will interest targeted media outlets.

Most public relations textbooks, including this one, emphasize systematic processes and logical structures. There's good reason for that. If a public relations plan is not thoroughly researched, well analyzed, and coherent, decision makers will not take it seriously. However, as mentioned in Chapter 3, logic and accuracy are only the foundation of a strong plan. A public relations plan also must be creative, fresh, and of interest to your target publics if you want it to succeed.

Persuasion in Public Relations

An underlying goal of most communication is persuasion at some level. Every day, we influence others to act, consider, believe, or attend to something in some way. For example, announcing that dinner will be served at 6 p.m. is not merely an informative message; it also persuades the receiver to behave in a certain way—to be at the table at 6 p.m. Similarly, all public relations messages have persuasive elements. We must influence a target public to first notice the message, then absorb its contents, and finally, to act on it. Clearly, with today's glut of persuasive messages on billboards, radios, televisions, websites, email blasts, social media, apparel, and printed materials, we must do something to make our messages stand out and be heard.

Consider, for example, that you are responsible for organizing an upscale, black-tie fundraising dinner and silent auction at a local hotel. Planning the event is only half the job. Just because you "build it" doesn't mean "they will come," no matter how wonderful or worthwhile your client thinks the event is. What will entice potential donors to attend? How is *this* nonprofit organization different from the hundreds of other charities one might sponsor? Why would someone attend *this* event over the many others that are held every month? Announcements and media alerts aren't enough. To engage the media and attract attendees, you need a special "hook" that appeals to your audience's unique self-interests. This is one reason why your research-based audience analysis is so important. A thorough and accurate understanding of the target public's values, interests, and motivations is essential to developing an effective persuasive strategy.

Similarly, secondary target publics for public relations often are the media. Your goal is to persuade various media outlets to accept and distribute your messages. This means you must develop a persuasive strategy based on a clear, research-based understanding of the motivations and values of each media outlet's readers, viewers, or listeners and craft newsworthy media materials. To develop your strategy, it's helpful to have some understanding of persuasion theory and of active and passive audiences.

Persuasion Theory

One particularly useful theory of persuasion for public relations is the Elaboration Likelihood Model (ELM), which was developed by Richard E. Petty and John T. Cacioppo (1981, 1986). This model proposes that people process persuasive messages through two routes: (1) the *central route* and (2) the *peripheral route.*

The *central route* to persuasion is the most direct. This route involves logical analysis and evaluation of the persuasive message by the receiver. This means the message must carry with it strong evidence and support. Persuasive messages for pharmaceutical products, for example, include evidence of efficacy, often in the form of scientific studies and testimonials.

The *peripheral route* to persuasion is an indirect path. It relies on the message receiver *elaborating* on message content by associating it with things that are positive and familiar. Celebrity endorsements, for example, aim at the peripheral route. When Michael Jordan recommends Hanes underwear, message receivers recognize his stellar NBA record and draw a positive association with the brand without examining or analyzing the message content. As always, understanding your audience is essential for determining which route to persuasion you want to take. Thus, it is helpful to consider publics as *active* or *passive.*

Grunig's Situational Theory of Publics

James Grunig's (1997) situational theory of publics is a helpful way to think about audiences and appropriate persuasive strategies to reach them. This theory proposes that target publics can be classified in terms of the extent to which they are aware of and ready to act on any given topic. *Active publics* are interested in the topic and are likely to seek detailed information on that subject. This means the central route to persuasion is effective for these people. Such tools as brochures, information packets, schematics, diagrams, and other materials that provide comprehensive information and background are appropriate for active publics. *Passive publics* may or may not be aware of the topic and have relatively little interest in it. For these publics, which are not likely to seek information, the *peripheral route* is more likely to be effective, and it should be accessed through short, repetitive messages, such as jingles, bumper stickers, and celebrity endorsements. Here, you are planting seeds and raising awareness, rather than providing detailed information for immediate action.

Active audiences can become passive and vice versa. Consider, for example, that you represent a refrigerator manufacturer. A newlywed couple plans to purchase their first refrigerator. This is a major expenditure, and the couple becomes part of an active public. They have a keen interest in the topic, and they are likely to visit stores, talk to friends, read reviews, and visit corporate websites to compare specifications and energy efficiency, check *Consumer Reports*, and seek advice. They will be persuaded to make their final decision based on facts and evidence—in other words, through the central route. Your job, then, is to provide persuasive evidence about your client's brand to these potential customers. However, the couple will not remain an active audience. Once they purchase the new fridge, their interest will wane.

Let's jump ahead five years. Our married couple is still happy with their refrigerator, and they have become part of a passive audience. They will not look for information on refrigerators. Detailed messages will not reach them, nor will this couple be interested in them. Instead, the peripheral route is more likely to be effective in grabbing their attention and stimulating positive associations with your client's brand of refrigerator. Eventually, when they need a new refrigerator, the couple will again become part of an active public. Then, those peripheral route tools can help persuade them to look at your client's information.

Identifying and distinguishing between active and passive audiences and the routes to persuasion for each is helpful because we can then develop appropriate types of tools to reach our audiences. The big question, of course, is how to develop an overarching creative strategy or make something newsworthy.

Persuasive Strategy: Developing the 'Big Idea'

As noted in the introduction to this text, strategies tie together all your tactics to form a unified, cohesive plan. The strategies you choose must be creative and fresh to be effective. This is not as difficult as it may at first appear, if you consider some underlying factors for creative approaches.

Sandra Moriarty, professor emerita of the University of Colorado, described what constitutes "the Big Idea" (1997). First, there is an element of risk. We must take a leap of faith beyond the safe, bland strategic statement and take our strategic concept to a new level that may be untried and unknown. In 2011, the Greater Houston Convention and Visitors Bureau did just that with its Public Relations Society of America Silver Anvil Award-winning "Where the Chefs Eat: Houston Culinary Tours" campaign. In an effort to promote Houston's culinary offerings and boost its reputation, these tours departed from traditional, behind-the-scenes tours of famous chefs' kitchens. Instead, the tour invited participants to visit restaurants where the chefs ate on their days off. This fresh approach resulted in every tour selling out within five minutes, with a waiting list of more than 1,500 people, as well as more than 11 million media impressions.

Second, as we have already discussed, the strategy must be relevant to the target audience and appeal to that audience's interests, values, and motivations. South Wales Fire and Rescue (2011) won a prestigious CIPR Excellence Award in 2011 for its "Project Bernie" campaign, which was designed to overcome an accepted local practice of setting grassfires each spring in the target area of Tonypandy. The audience was young males who perceived the annual ritual as fairly "harmless." These youth were reached by forming a Youth Advisory Board of teens from a local college. The students developed Bernie the Sheep, a cartoon mascot, along with the tag line "Grass is Green, Fire is Mean." The program was so successful that it was extended to three additional areas in South Wales.

Big ideas are designed to solve communication problems. If they are not strategic then they are not Big Ideas, but rather just random thoughts.

~Professor Sandra Moriarty

Third, the Big Idea must have a recognizable emotional, physical, or intellectual impact on the target public. Edelman and Starbucks Coffee Company won a 2011 PRSA Silver Anvil with the Starbucks Coffee Company Earth Month campaign, which did that. Edelman and Starbucks recognized that environment was the #1 concern of consumers, and that people trusted brands with ethical and socially responsible reputations. Starbucks, in an effort to enhance its reputation for being environmentally conscious, engaged its customers during its April 2010 "Earth Month" through a five-milestone strategy that included, among other things, offering free coffee to customers with a reusable mug or tumbler, convening a "Second Cup Summit" to work toward a recyclable cup solution, and facilitating speaking engagements at conferences about environmental stewardship. More than 1.2 million consumers participated in the tumbler promotion, and Starbucks saw its reputation as an environmentally responsible organization measurably enhanced.

Finally, to be truly "big," the Big Idea must be original. One example of originality is the "Expedition 206" campaign from Coca-Cola and Fast Horse, which won a PRSA Silver Anvil Award of Excellence. This unprecedented global campaign aimed to send

FIGURE 4-1
While the concept of a Big Idea may seem daunting at first, it really is a matter of allowing yourself to think freely about the client's goals and how they mesh with those of your target publics.

© 2012 by ra2 studio. Used under license of Shutterstock, Inc.

three young people to nearly 206 countries in a one-year period as part of Coca-Cola's "Open Happiness" campaign. The travelers used both social and traditional media from each country they visited to tell their stories, generating more than 60,000 YouTube viewers and making a personal connection with millions of consumers on an international basis. A word of caution about originality: It may take some research to verify that your idea is unusual and imaginative. Although something may be new to you and your team, it may be old hat to others.

Brainstorming, surfing the Internet, looking at what has been done before for similar projects, and considering new twists can help you develop that Big Idea. Brainstorming, per se, tends to be less productive than a method known as the *nominal group technique*, first proposed in 1971 by André L. Delbecq and Andrew H. Van de Ven. This approach facilitates open discussion and encourages equal contributions from all team members. The following steps present a condensed form of this technique:

1. **Develop and state the question**. Everyone needs to agree on this as a starting point for discussion. It may be something like "How can we help the client attain the goal of improving employee morale?" or "What is the best strategy to appeal to this target audience?"

2. **Work independently**. Each team member spends some time alone, developing as many ideas as possible that answer the stated question.

3. **Gather ideas**. Record all ideas on a flipchart, whiteboard, or some other medium that is visible to all team members. Each person provides one idea at a time, which can be revised with permission from the team.

4. **Discussion**. Avoiding all judgments of value or merit, discuss and clarify each idea. The outcome of this step should be a concise list of ideas for further consideration.

5. **Prioritize ideas**. Limiting the number to no more than 5–8 ideas, identify those of top priority by having team members vote. If there are many ideas, it might help to categorize them. For example, categories might be "most cost effective," "best overall strategy," or "most appropriate for client's organizational culture." This step also includes clarifying any misunderstandings, and allowing team members to change their minds, if they choose.

6. **Discuss implications**. Develop the intended and unintended consequences of the chosen ideas, how they can be implemented, and how well they address the client's goals.

Beyond brainstorming, considering some basic principles of newsworthiness can help get you there, as well.

Newsworthiness

Novice practitioners often make the mistake of thinking that if they use the proper format and style of a news release, the media will run with it. However, a perfectly written but dull release will never see print. A release must be newsworthy, preferably from a variety of perspectives, but especially from the perspective of the media outlet's audiences.

Six criteria of newsworthiness can help you craft both effective news releases and creative strategies for your public relations program. They are:

1. Prominence

2. Timeliness

3. Proximity

4. Impact

5. Conflict

6. Novelty

Prominence refers to a person, place, or thing that is well known or important. Celebrity status, political power, fame, or notoriety can create prominence. Keep the consumers of each media outlet in mind when determining prominence. For example, the mayor of a small town may be prominent and newsworthy for a local paper, but not for national media. Similarly, celebrity magazines might be interested in Lindsay Lohan's shopping sprees, but political media are not. Consider, too, that prominence, alone, may or may not be enough to make a story newsworthy.

Timeliness means the story is recent or is connected in some way to a current trend. Sometimes this can be cyclical, so it's helpful to look at media trends. For example, each January we can observe media interest in fitness and weight loss methods as people establish resolutions for the New Year. The weight loss and fitness industries have known this for years. As a result, we see them launch new programs and major campaigns during the first couple of months each year.

Proximity is the physical location of the story. The closer a story is geographically to a media outlet's consumers, the more newsworthy it is likely to be. For example, a fundraising golf outing at a local golf course will most likely be of interest only to local papers unless additional newsworthy elements are in place, such as a *prominent* golfer or celebrity.

Impact refers to the consequences of the story. Here, you are concerned with how many people the story will affect. The larger the impact, the higher the likelihood that the story is viewed as newsworthy. A river overflowing its banks, for example, may only be of interest to a few people, if it does no damage. However, if it threatens homes, the story becomes newsworthy. Major floods that affect large areas and displace many people can become national and even international news.

Conflict tends to capture people's attention. The old saying that "if it bleeds, it leads" holds true. We tend to think of conflict as wars, protests, and the like. But conflict can be developed linguistically, as well, as it was with the U.S. government's "War on Drugs," which was part of the Comprehensive Drug Abuse Prevention and Control Act of 1970. Public relations professionals also use manufactured conflicts such as competitions and contests to bring an element of excitement and newsworthiness to a campaign.

FIGURE 4-2
Conflict, particularly if it is close to the target public (proximity) or affects many people (impact) is often newsworthy.

© 2012 by Jbor studio . Used under license of Shutterstock, Inc.

Novelty or uniqueness is a key element in newsworthiness. This is where your Big Idea is important. First, last, biggest, tallest, oldest, youngest—superlatives refer to things that are unique. Try to incorporate events and story ideas into your public relations program that involve unusual elements to increase newsworthiness.

Tying It All Together

Public relations is inherently persuasive. While PR must be systematic and logical, it also must have a creative edge to appeal to target publics. A "Big Idea" is a fresh, new approach that is both relevant to and impacts your target publics.

One way to create an identity for your campaign is to develop a theme for your public relations program. It might center on a tagline or a catchy campaign identification or a unique character, like a mascot. This theme might be an innovative activity or contest or story. Whatever device you use, it must directly (1) appeal to your target public based on careful audience analysis, and (2) address your client's goals. The concepts of newsworthiness can also help with the development of the Big Idea, as well as appeal to media.

None of the characteristics of newsworthiness stand alone. The more elements of newsworthiness you can incorporate into a story, the more newsworthy it is likely to be. This means that when you're thinking of something *unique*, also consider ways in which you can increase *impact*, localize it for *proximity* to your target publics, draw interest with *prominent* people or organizations, and *time* it to current trends or events.

Name _____ Date _____

REFLECT AND REVIEW

1. You are a public affairs specialist for a small liberal arts college, which has just named a new president. You are charged with announcing the appointment to the media. Which media would you target and why?

   _____

   _____

   _____

   _____

2. Your client, a small printing company, is entering its 10th year of business and wants to do "something special" to celebrate a decade of success. The target is the general public in the local area, a highly diverse audience. Is this an active or passive public? Justify your answer.

   Passive, not everybody might be interested in the printing company & its "something special

   _____

3. Which of the following tools is best suited to reach an active audience? Justify your answer in terms of the Elaboration Likelihood Model of persuasion.

   - Feature article _____

   - Brochure _____

   - Door hanger _____

   - Website _____

   - Table tent _____

4. You work for Wonder Widgets, a huge manufacturing firm with corporate offices in New York. Of the six items below, which is the most likely to be considered newsworthy by local New York papers? Would any be better targeted to national newspapers? Would you send any to multiple outlets? What would you suggest be done to improve the newsworthiness of each item? Be specific and justify your answer in terms of the criteria for newsworthiness outlined in the text.

   i.   Wonder's annual employee recognition dinner in two months.

   ii. The promotion of Wonder's vice president of engineering to senior vice president of research and development.

   iii. The death of East Livingston, NJ resident F. Fieldstone, one of Wonder's longtime employees.

   iv. Wonder's quarterly earnings statement.

   v.   The Laguna Beach, CA wedding of Wonder's president and CEO.

   vi. The latest information on Wonder's newest and innovative widget.

   _____

   _____

   _____

   _____

   _____

   _____

CHAPTER 4 REFERENCES AND RESOURCES

Delbecq A. L., & Van de Ven, A. H. (1971). A group process model for problem identification and program planning. *Journal of Applied Behavioral Science, VII,*
466–491.

Diehl, M., & Stroebe, W. (1987). Productivity loss in brainstorming groups: Toward the
solution of a riddle. *Journal of Personality and Social Psychology, 53*(3), 497–509.

Fast Horse. (2011). *Fast Horse and Coke engage the world.* Retrieved from http://
fasthorseinc.com/home/fast-horse-portfolio/clients/coca-cola/expedition206

Fast Horse & The Coca-Cola Company. (2011). *Coca-Cola's Expedition 206.* Retrieved
from http://www.prsa.org/SearchResults/Download/6BE-1102C07

Geisel, T. S. (Dr. Seuss). (1975). *Oh, the thinks you can think!* New York: Random
House.

Greater Houston Convention and Visitors Bureau. (2011). *Houston culinary tours.*
Public Relations Society of America Silver Anvil Awards. Retrieved from http://
www.prsa.org/SearchResults/Download/6BW-1102D01

Grunig, J. E. (1997). A situational theory of publics: Conceptual history, recent challenges and new research. In D. Moss, T. MacManus, & D. Vercic (Eds.), *Public
relations research: An international perspective* (pp. 3–48). London: International
Thomson Business Press.

Moriarty, S. E. (1997). The big idea: Creativity in public relations. In C. L. Caywood
(Ed.), *The handbook of strategic public relations and integration.* (pp. 554–563).
New York: McGraw-Hill.

Petty, R. E., & Cacioppo, J. T. (1981). A*ttitudes and persuasion: Classic and contemporary approaches.* Dubuque, IA: Wm. C. Brown.

Petty, R. E., & Cacioppo, J. T. (1986). *Communication and persuasion: Central and
peripheral routes to attitude change.* New York: Springer-Verlag.

South Wales Fire & Rescue Service. (2011). *Project Bernie.* Chartered Institute of Public
Relations Excellence Awards. Retrieved from http://www.cipr.co.uk/sites/default/
files/Project%20Bernie.pdf

Starbucks Coffee Company & Edelman. (2011). *Starbucks Coffee Company earth month.*
Retrieved from http://www.prsa.org/SearchResults/Download/6BE-1107E03

Chapter 5

Writing the Public Relations Plan:
Step 1 Research

There is nothing like looking, if you want to find something. ... You certainly usually find something, if you look, but it is not always quite the something you were after.

~ J. R. R. Tolkien

This chapter addresses the importance of both formative and summative research for public relations in planning and implementing a program and in evaluating program effectiveness. It introduces readers to primary and secondary research tools for audience analysis, situation analysis, organizational analysis, and program evaluation and impact. The chapter also includes some special considerations for incorporating research into a public relations plan.

LEARNING OBJECTIVES

The information presented in this chapter will enable you to:

1. Distinguish between formative and summative research.

2. Distinguish between primary and secondary research.

3. Distinguish between qualitative and quantitative research methods.

4. Define *reliability*, *validity*, and *generalizability*.

5. Conduct effective keyword searches.

6. Appraise resources for credibility, accuracy, reasonableness, and support.

7. Select appropriate research methods that answer specific questions to plan and evaluate public relations programs and their effects.

As discussed in Chapter 1, although research is the first of the four-step public relations process, we really conduct research throughout an entire project. It's never truly finished.

We begin with questions. We ask, among other things, questions about the client, the client's environment, the client's goals, the client's competition, and the client's market niche. Formative research helps us answer these and other questions before the plan is developed or implemented. New questions arise throughout planning and implementation, and they require more research. At the completion of the program, we have still more questions, such as the extent to which we reached our objectives or whether audience behaviors or attitudes were altered by our messages. We use summative research in the evaluation step to answer this new set of questions. For these reasons, it's helpful to think of the research and evaluation steps as matching bookends to any public relations plan.

The research tools you choose depend on the information you need to know, so you should develop your question before you select a research method. For example, if you want to determine the readability of a message, you would not find the answer in the library or on the Internet; you would use a readability index, such as *Flesch-Kincaid Grade Level Test, Flesch Reading Ease Test, Gunning Fog Index*, or *Fry Readability Formula*. (Many word processing programs, including Microsoft Word for both PC and Mac, can be set to check readability with one or more of these tools.) Your goal may be to establish credibility with decision makers, define and segment target publics, formulate your strategies and tactics, or test messages. Whatever the purpose, you need to be able to critically read research reports, as well as develop your own research agendas.

This chapter outlines a few of the most commonly used research methods in PR. Many resources are devoted to describing detailed methodologies, including Professor Earl R. Babbie's excellent 2010 book, *The Practice of Social Research*, which is listed in the references for this chapter. Before we examine specific research methods, though, we need to understand some of the terms that researchers use.

The Language of Research

Research methods are categorized and discussed within a variety of contexts. Some research is *informal*. It is not highly structured, tends to be exploratory, and does not follow specific rules. Examples of informal research include informational interviews with knowledgeable staff, gathering anecdotal information, and consideration of past experiences.

"Normally, this project would require weeks of research and verification...but luckily there's an app for it."

Formal research requires that data are gathered and structured according to accepted rules, such as in experimental studies. This chapter focuses on formal research methods. One category that is particularly pertinent to the practice of public relations is *formative* versus *summative* research. These two terms address the general purpose of the research.

Formative and Summative Research

Formative research is done before a public relations program is implemented and is often exploratory in nature. (Think of *forming* the program plan.) Activities such as feasibility studies, audience analysis, baseline survey studies of attitudes or awareness, and information gathered for PEST and SWOT analyses constitute formative research. Formative research also may be used to test the effectiveness or audience acceptance of messages before widespread distribution.

Summative research is used to evaluate the success of a public relations program (think of *sum*mations, which typically occur at the end of legal argument). Summative research is done in the evaluation step of the public relations process, and it determines the extent to which objectives were met. Examples include post-campaign survey studies to determine attitudinal or awareness changes resulting from a public relations program, counting press clippings, calculating media impressions, and measuring audience behaviors.

Primary and Secondary Research

Both formative and summative research may be either primary or secondary. *Secondary* research is information that has been collected and reported by others. If you use the Web or a library to look up U.S. Census data or scan databases to learn about a client and competing organizations, you are conducting secondary research. This type of research is usually done during the research and planning steps of the public relations process, which means it is part of your formative research strategy.

Primary research is that which you personally conduct. You collect the data, you analyze it, and you report it in some way, usually in the form of a written document. For example, interviewing the client for background information is a form of primary research. Another example is surveying a target public to measure awareness of your client's organization. This might be done before the program is implemented as formative research to determine a baseline measure, and then after program completion to see if there has been a change in awareness. All primary research, whether it is formative or summative, is either qualitative or quantitative or a hybrid of the two methodologies.

Qualitative and Quantitative Research

Quantitative research, as the name implies, involves quantities or numerical measures of some sort. Any research that yields "hard" data or analyses in the form of numbers or statistics, such as frequencies or percentages, is quantitative. This research aims to be both *verifiable* and *reliable*, and should be *generalizable* to an entire population when drawn from samples. For example, Gallup polls use carefully structured samples to determine awareness, opinions, and attitudes of various publics.

Imagine that you are trying to understand the character of a lawn. Your quantitative research might count the number of blades of grass per square inch, measure the color of the grass with a color chart, and the number of weeds per square foot. All these things investigate the surface and general appearance of the *entire* lawn. Similarly, quantitative research in public relations tells us something about an industry or client or audience, such as how many people in an area are aware of a client's product or how often people visit a museum exhibit. Examples of quantitative research methods for public relations include surveys and content analyses.

Qualitative research involves asking questions that are not easily answered with numbers, such as people's experiences and values. It yields "soft" data that is *verifiable*, but not necessarily *reliable*. Where quantitative research looks at such things as general trends or opinions, qualitative research investigates underlying explanations or characteristics. Examples of qualitative research for public relations include focus groups and interviews.

Returning to our analogy of studying a lawn, instead of gathering data about the surface of the entire lawn, as is done with quantitative research, qualitative research cores down into the soil to see if the roots are dry or if cutworms are present. The results may only be accurate for the areas that were cored, so they are not generalizable to the entire lawn, but they still provide valuable information about the nature of the lawn.

Reliability, Validity, and Generalizability

Whether you are designing your own research protocol (primary research) or reading a research report (secondary research), it is essential that you look at the design with a critical eye to be able to discern its accuracy and objectivity. Understanding reliability, validity, and generalizability helps you make intelligent decisions about conducting your own research or analyzing the research reports produced by others.

Reliability refers to the extent to which a research method is consistent across multiple studies. A reliable research protocol will yield similar results every time it is done. Medical and pharmaceutical studies must be highly reliable because the lives of many people depend on the results. Quantitative methods in public relations research should be reliable. Qualitative methods in public relations may not always be reliable, because we often are dealing with opinions, which change over time and across groups of people. For example, the opinions of a focus group this year may be quite different next year.

Validity (specifically, *internal validity*) means that the research measures what it claims to measure. Obviously, you wouldn't use a yardstick as the sole instrument to measure the weight of an object, because the measurement would not be *valid*. By the same token, we need to use appropriate forms of measurement when examining opinions, awareness, or other social phenomena. Both qualitative and quantitative methods must be valid.

Generalizability (which relates to *external validity*) is a term that indicates the extent to which a study's results can be generalized to a larger population. For example, if you are planning survey research to determine opinions of all residents in the state of California, time and budget undoubtedly would dictate that you use a sample of California residents, rather than the entire population. The sample, therefore, must be demographically and psychographically representative of the entire population being studied to be generalizable. Reliability, validity, and generalizability all depend, at least in part, on how the elements of a study are *operationalized*.

Operationalization

Operationalization involves defining the concepts or variables of your research in a way that they are both observable and measurable. For example, we might operationalize a quantity of water by defining it in terms of milliliters as measured by pouring it into a graduated cylinder. Note that this operationalization spells out both the measure (milliliters) and the measurement tool (graduated cylinder). In social scientific research, operationalizing concepts or variables can be difficult. In fact, we seldom do a perfect job of operationalizing variables, but it is especially important to be as precise and thorough as possible to yield valid results.

So far, we've developed a rudimentary vocabulary for research. Our next step is to explore ways to gather information.

Finding the Answers to Your Questions

There are several good models that categorize public relations research according to purpose, and most share significant similarities. This text uses Professor Jim R. Macnamara's Pyramid Model of PR Research (2011; 2002), which is shown in Figure 5-1, because it helps pair the types of questions we might ask with appropriate research methodologies to answer them.

The Pyramid model is read from the bottom up. The base represents the foundation of the public relations process, when a huge amount of information must be gathered and analyzed. The Pyramid top represents the program outcomes, which are usually attitudinal or behavioral changes. Together, the Pyramid base, center, and capstone roughly track the public relations process and list the types of research questions asked at each stage of the research. The left side of the Pyramid depicts three general categories for which research is done, drawing on the language of systems theory:

1. Inputs: Strategic and physical *decisions*, such as the channel chosen to reach target publics

2. Outputs: Physical *materials and activities* produced as part of the public relations program, such as events or news articles

3. Outcomes: Attitudinal and behavioral *effects* or impact of the communication, such as the perceived reputation of the organization or adoption rates of new products

FIGURE 5-1 Macnamara's Pyramid Model of PR Research (2002, p. 85).

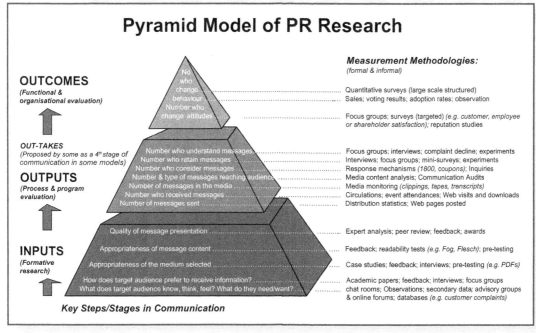

The right side of the Pyramid lists examples of appropriate research methodologies for each of the three classifications listed on the left. Note that formative research and summative research are purposely combined in this model because the research is seen as an integrated, constant flow of communication and feedback, rather than as discrete functions.

The metaphor of a pyramid is also useful to symbolise what I have argued for more than a decade—that is, more research should be done at the beginning and in the early stages of communication than at the end.

~*Jim R. Macnamara* (p. 16)

One notable advantage of the Pyramid Model of PR Research is that it provides a "starter" list of research methodologies to answer specific questions. However, once you have determined what to ask and appropriate methodologies to gather information that will answer your questions, a new question arises: How the heck *do* I do this? The following sections provide some introductory concepts and resources to get you started.

Conducting Secondary Research

As noted above, secondary research involves accessing information that others have gathered and archived. Secondary research is often the first thing that's done as part of your formative research to learn about the client and its environment. Internet search engines, such as Google or Yahoo! or Bing, may be helpful, but don't stop there. Local or specialized or academic libraries, which are usually affiliated with colleges and universities, as well as the Internet, offer many excellent online and offline resources. Forethought and care are necessary for this type of research. While it might seem easy to throw a few words into a search box, doing *effective* searches is something of an art.

How To Do Effective Searches

There's more to searching than just throwing in words or phrases. In fact, entering words or phrases incorrectly can scuttle an otherwise good research effort. Every search engine and every database has specific rules, so it's always wise to check the "advanced search" options to be sure you are entering the information in the most effective manner. There are six commonly used types of searches:

1. Boolean searches

2. Field searches

3. Phrase searches

4. Keyword in context (KWIC) searches

5. Proximity searches

6. Truncation searches

Each type of search yields specific results. The following sections briefly look at each in turn:

Boolean Searches. The Boolean search is the oldest, simplest, and most widely used type of search structure. It uses "and," "or," and "not" operators. For example, if you are looking for information on the history of teddy bears, you might enter the words "teddy bear." The results will yield all documents that contain either the word "teddy" or "bear." This means you'll have to wade through millions of documents about many unrelated topics, including Teddy Pendergrass or Smokey the Bear or Teddy Roosevelt or Bear Mountain Ski Resort.

The Boolean search can be narrowed a bit by using the operators. For example, you can type "teddy AND bear," which means the results must include both terms somewhere in the text. Additional precision can be incorporated by adding the "not" variable, such as "teddy AND bear NOT cartoon." However, this method still can yield results unrelated to your research question.

Field Searches. Field searches allow you to specify where the words should appear, such as a title or author in a database search or a URL, headers, or links in a Web-based search. Thus, if you are searching online for information on the history of teddy bears, you could specify the field in which your key words would appear.

Phrase Searches. Some search operations allow you to use phrases as a default or by delineating the phrase with quotation marks, such as "teddy bear." You need to check the search instructions to be sure if and how such search terms are processsed, but this typically works with Boolean searches, as well, such as searching for "teddy bear" AND "history." The results will yield documents that contain the phrase "teddy bear" and the word "history" anywhere in the text.

Keyword in Context Searches. KWIC searches define the context in which the search terms should appear by specifying words that appear near your primary search terms. For example, you might search for "teddy bear" with "history" as a contextual keyword. The results will be documents in which the word "history" appears physically near the phrase "teddy bear."

Proximity Searches. Similar to KWIC searches, proximity searches narrow your results by specifying a word or term to appear near your primary search term. However, such searches restrict the results even more, because you indicate the range of words within which the contextual word appears. For example, you might search for "teddy bear" within five words of "history."

Truncation Searches. Properly used, truncation searches can be among the most useful when you have a term with many possible variations. The word "communication," for example, might be used in a variety of ways, depending on the author and context. If you think variations on the word are likely, a truncation search can solve the problem by using a "wild card" symbol to indicate unknown characters. For example, using an asterisk as the wild card, a search of "communic*" will yield results for "communication," "communicative," "communicate," "communicates," "communicated," and "communicating."

A careful strategy for database and Web searching is necessary to find the information you need. However, no single technique will "do it all." A number of search engines also have special features that help you improve your search. It therefore pays to use a variety of search methods and *double check the advanced search features of the search engine or database you are accessing*. The more narrowly you can focus your search, the better your results.

As you formulate your search strategy, try to think of words unique to the topic. Look for relevance reports of your results when the search is on the Web. That helps you see the applicability of the results to your keywords. Once found, you also need to discern the quality of the information you have gathered. Not all public information is useful, especially when you've found it on the Internet.

Tips For Evaluating Resources

One way to evaluate the quality of Internet resources is to apply Dr. Robert Harris's *CARS Checklist* (Credibility, Accuracy, Reasonableness, Support). Although the checklist was originally developed for evaluation of online materials, it is equally useful for offline resources:

- **Credibility**. Is the source credible? Look for author credentials, professional position, education, or experience. If the material is produced by an organization, consider organizational reputation. Generally, government, educational, and nonprofit institutions are credible resources. Scholarly works published through a peer review process usually provide excellent information. Beware of anonymous resources, resources that have received negative reviews, and materials with multiple errors in grammar and spelling.

- **Accuracy**. Is the information correct and up to date? Look for comprehensive, well-documented facts. Consider why and for whom the information was produced. Objective information is presented far differently than information in persuasive messages. For example, an article on the efficacy of toothbrushes that is written by a toothbrush company may well be biased in favor of the company's style of toothbrush. Check for lack of accuracy by looking for sweeping generalizations, undated material, information that may be out of date, and unacknowledged opposing views.

- **Reasonableness**. Does the information seem fair, objective, moderate, and consistent? Consider whether the information is balanced and reasoned, presenting both sides of an argument. If the material is emotional, it is probably seeking a peripheral route to persuasion, rather than informing. Consider, too, how moderate the information is. If it appears hard to believe or unlikely, look for supporting evidence from other sources. Also, consider consistency throughout the material. Contradictions or inconsistencies can indicate poor-quality information.

- **Support**. Is the material supported by other sources? Look for in-text citations of credible sources and full bibliographic information. Seek additional, corroborating sources to verify the material. Numbers or statistics that have no attributions or corroborating resources may be inaccurate or false. Be especially careful to look at the writing. Many websites simply replicate, word-for-word, information from other websites. *Identical writing without appropriate attribution indicates plagiarism, not corroboration.*

Finding Information about Organizations

Recall the Chapter 1 discussion of systems theory and of organizations as open social systems. To write the situation analysis as described in Chapter 3, you must understand your client (or potential client) and the client's system components, internal processes, and environmental influences. That means you have to assemble a lot of information for your situation analysis.

Nonsubscription Databases. Visits to a potential client's website can certainly be useful. The website will most likely give you some basic information about the organization. However, there is also a lot of information that organizational websites

TABLE 5-1: Summary of Dr. Robert Harris's *CARS Checklist for Research Source Evaluation*.	
Credibility	Trustworthy source, author's credentials, evidence of quality control, known or respected authority, organizational support. *Goal:* An authoritative source, a source that supplies some good evidence that allows you to trust it.
Accuracy	Up to date, factual, detailed, exact, comprehensive, audience and purpose reflect intentions of completeness and accuracy. *Goal:* A source that is correct today (not yesterday), a source that gives the whole truth.
Reasonableness	Fair, balanced, objective, reasoned, no conflict of interest, absence of fallacies or slanted tone. *Goal:* A source that engages the subject thoughtfully and reasonably, concerned with the truth.
Support	Listed sources, contact information, available corroboration, claims supported, documentation supplied. *Goal:* A source that provides convincing evidence for the claims made, a source you can triangulate (find at least two other sources that support it).

are *not* likely to have, such as operating revenues, competitive businesses, and consumer complaints. Such websites as *Yelp* (http://www.yelp.com), *MRI+* (http://www.mriplus.com), and *Trip Advisor* (http://www.tripadvisor.com) list reviews and ratings posted by consumers. Many shopping websites, such as *Amazon* (http://www.amazon.com) and *Price Grabber* (http://www.pricegrabber.com) also include customer ratings and reviews.

Subscription and Proprietary Databases. For larger organizations, subscription databases, such as *Hoover's* (http://www.hoovers.com), *Associations Unlimited* (published by Gale, http://www.gale.cengage.com), *Standard and Poor's* (http://www.standardandpoors.com), and *Mint* (http://www.mintportal.bvdep.com) offer first-rate information. In addition, you may want to see what the media are saying about the organization and its competitors by doing keyword searches for the company in *Lexis-Nexis* (http://www.lexisnexis.com), *ABI/Inform* through Proquest (http://www.proquest.com/products/pt-product-ABI.shtml) and in business magazine databases, such as *Business Source Premier* or *Business Full Text* from EBSCO Publishing (http://www.ebscohost.com).

You can also gather basic, introductory information on many topics and organizations through online encyclopedias and dictionaries. However, be cautious and carefully evaluate the quality of online resources. For example, a 2008 study by Lucy Holman Rector reported that the accuracy rate of *Wikipedia* was only 80%, while that of *Encyclopaedia Britannica*, *The Dictionary of American History*, and *American National Biography Online* was 95–96%. Wikipedia has taken steps to improve this statistic, but it does not yet carry the same credibility as some other online encyclopedias. One excellent place to start is *CQ Researcher* (http://library.cqpress.com/cqresearcher), which provides comprehensive information on current issues, beginning with an overview and background, and then focusing more narrowly on objective analysis.

Beyond understanding the client, its industry, and its environment, you will need extensive information on potential audiences. Everything you put into your plan hinges on clearly understanding audience interests, values, influencers, and motivations.

Finding Information about Potential Publics

Information on potential publics can be categorized as *demographic* or *psychographic*. Demographic information, which describes statistical characteristics of groups of people, is certainly useful. These data commonly include such information as age, gender, ethnicity, geographic area, salary range, and education. Sometimes demographic variables are considered in terms of generational cohorts, such as *Baby Boomers*, *Gen Xers*, and *Millennials*. Demographics can provide some insight about the general culture of a group of people, but demographic information doesn't tell the whole story. To develop a truly effective strategy, you need to understand the psychographics of the people you hope to target, as well.

Psychographic analyses look at such attributes as lifestyles, interests, attitudes, personalities, and values. Solid audience analysis results in a psychographic profile of a target public. For example, consider a hypothetical target public comprised of married couples in the age range of 25–35 with college-level educations and living in Indianapolis, Indiana. If you rely purely on the demographics, you might use the same strategies, tactics, and tools for the entire public—and that would be a huge mistake. Let's look at three possible psychographic variations in this group: (1) the Double-Income, No Kids group (DINKS), (2) the Single-Income, No Kids group (SINKS), and (3) the Married with Kids group. Each psychographic cluster is likely to have different interests and motivations. Their lifestyles and values are wildly divergent. They do not read, listen to, or view the same media. That means you must develop different objectives, strategies, tactics, and tools for each psychographic profile. Fortunately, there are a variety of tools to help you develop a psychographic profile of your audience, both online and offline.

Offline Resources. The *New Strategist* series of books, which can be ordered online at http://www.newstrategist.com or accessed through some libraries, has excellent information on American consumerism, including socioeconomic and spending characteristics of ethnic groups, generation cohort guides, and more. Research libraries also are likely to have population databases, such as those from the U.S. Census and Rand Corporation.

Online Resources. The U.S. Department of Labor, Bureau of Labor Statistics (http://www.bls.gov) has many resources concerning the U.S. workforce, including unemployment rates, productivity, strikes, lockouts, and more. The Consumer Expenditure Survey (http://www.bls.gov/cex) is a free database drawn from the Quarterly Interview Survey and the Diary Survey to deliver information on U.S. consumer buying habits. The U.S. Census Bureau (http://www.census.gov) also offers a great deal of information on American employment, demographics, and consumerism. These types of information help you determine which media are most appropriate to reach your target publics.

Finding Information about Media

Whether you use online or offline resources to develop your media contact lists, double-check that the information is up to date. People change jobs quickly in both print and broadcast media, and sending your material to an editor or journalist who has moved on can cost you the placement.

Offline Resources. A number of directories are available to help you identify local, national, and even international media outlets. *Bacon's Media Directories* for newspapers, television, and radio provide information on more than 250,000 editors, reporters, and columnists. The *Gale Directory of Publications and Broadcast Media* also has listings for thousands of print and broadcast outlets. The *Broadcasting &*

Cable Yearbook can help identify local cable companies, which will sometimes "bicycle" public service announcements (PSAs) around from company to company within a defined geographic area.

Online Resources. Many online marketing and PR resources track media outlets, but three fee-based websites are particularly worth exploring. *Vocus* (http://www.vocus.com) offers cloud-based software that provides a database of media, bloggers, and influencers. *Vocus* also monitors blogs and social media and provides measurable analyses of public relations efforts. *Cision* (http://www.cision.com) produces *Bacon's Media Directories*. Its online products include an extensive media database, press release distribution, and media monitoring and analysis. *BurellesLuce* (http://www.burellesluce.com) also offers excellent information on media contacts, monitoring, and reporting, including social media.

Beyond answering preliminary questions, secondary research also may serve as a springboard for your primary research. Answers to some of your questions, such as levels of audience awareness, require primary research methods.

Conducting Primary Research

One of the most obvious places to begin your research is to simply talk to the client. An informal, conversational *unstructured interview* allows maximum flexibility and provides the interviewee with opportunities to take the conversation in directions that you may not have considered. This effort can yield excellent qualitative information and guide you to additional ideas or resources, such as existing organizational materials, files, and key stakeholders. However, as Macnamara's Pyramid illustrates, many questions might require primary research.

Whether you are conducting qualitative or quantitative research, you'll probably need to *sample* the population in which you're interested. We rarely have either the time or the budget to gather information from every member of a public, so a few words about sampling are in order.

Sampling Methods

When you taste a sample of ice cream, you expect a full scoop to taste the same as the sample. In other words, the sample should be representative of the entire batch. Similarly, when you draw a sample for social research, you need to be sure the sample is representative of the entire group of people in which you are interested. This means the sample must be representative of an entire population, whether the population in question is everyone in a broad geographic area or people within a narrowly defined set of characteristics.

There are two general categories of sampling methods: *probability sampling* and *nonprobability sampling*. Probability sampling is done in such a way that each individual has the same likelihood of being included. Nonprobability sampling involves some decision about the selection, which causes an uneven likelihood of inclusion in the sample, and excludes some individuals. Figure 5-2 depicts a partial list of probability and nonprobability sampling methods. We address a few of those methods here.

Probability Sampling. The *simple random sample* must be drawn in such a way that every individual in the population of interest has an equal chance of being selected. For example, if you want to sample 100 individuals who use your product, you might put everyone's name in a basket and randomly draw 100 names. Every name in the basket has an equal chance of being drawn, regardless of where they live, their occupations, or other variables. One useful technique is to assign numbers to all members of the population and then select the sample by using a random number

FIGURE 5-2. Probability samples are drawn so every member of the population has an equal chance to be included.

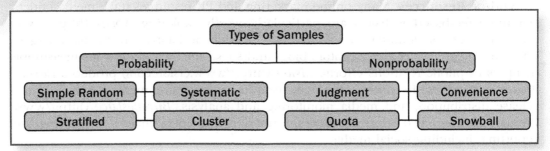

generator. There are several free random number generators available on the Web, including those at *Random.org* (http://www.random.org) and *Research Randomizer* (http://www.randomizer.org).

The term *random sample* is often misused by novice researchers. For example, standing on a corner on a Tuesday morning for an hour and interviewing passersby is *not* random. You are only speaking with people who cross that particular corner at that particular time. People who might cross the corner in the afternoon or on Wednesdays—or not at all—have no chance of being selected. You therefore need to consider carefully your population and the most cost-effective technique for drawing a simple random sample.

You might have reason to add some sort of pattern to a random sample. This technique is a *systematic random sample*. For example, you could number all the names in the population, randomly choose a starting number, and then select names based on specific intervals until you have drawn 100 individuals, perhaps every 10th name. This type of sampling, if not carefully thought through, can result in sampling bias, if the interval used happens to coincide with periodic variations in the population.

Nonprobability Sampling. *Convenience sampling* is also known as accidental or opportunity sampling. This technique involves drawing a sample on the basis of accessibility or convenience, rather than representativeness of the population in question. While convenience sampling is not usually appropriate for full research programs, it is useful and acceptable under certain conditions, such as a pilot study to test a survey instrument.

Judgment sampling is based on the judgment of the researcher. For example, when studying the population of a large geographic area, a smaller, representative area may be chosen from which to draw the sample. Making sound judgments that will not compromise the integrity of the study obviously requires significant expertise and knowledge. Whichever sampling technique you choose, you need to report it as part of your research methodology in your public relations plan. Of course, your sample depends, at least in part, on the nature of the research method you plan to use.

Qualitative Research Methods

Public relations professionals use a variety of formalized qualitative methods, including *structured*, *semi-structured*, and *unstructured interviews* of consumers, potential target publics, and organizational stakeholders; *advisory groups* of individuals with appropriate expertise; and *focus groups* of individuals who are representative of the target public. The following sections provide an overview of structured interviews and focus groups.

Structured Interviews. Gathering high-quality, dependable information through interviews requires some preparation. Your first requirement is to have a clear goal. Know exactly what information you need to gather and ask only questions that will provide it. Prepare a face sheet to record the date, time, location, participant names, and interview questions that will be asked of all participants. If you will have more than one interviewer, some training will be needed to ensure consistency of data collection. Strive to construct questions that are not biased or confusing or ask more than one thing. Here are some examples of question types to avoid:

- *Leading Question*: "Don't you agree that vehicle traffic congestion in this city is a problem?" This is a leading question. It leads the respondent toward the interviewer's point of view that traffic is a problem. Remove bias with neutral wording: "Is vehicle traffic congestion in this city a problem?"

- *Double-Barreled Question*: "Are pedestrian and vehicle traffic congestion in this city a problem?" This really asks two questions in one. The respondent may think pedestrian traffic is a problem, but not vehicle traffic, or vice versa. It should be split into two questions: "Is pedestrian traffic congestion in this city a problem?" and "Is vehicle traffic congestion in this city a problem?"

- *Confusing or wordy questions*: "What do you think about traffic in this city?" This question is unclear. Are you asking about traffic volume? Vehicle or pedestrian traffic? Traffic safety? This question is much less ambiguous: "Do you believe that vehicle traffic congestion in this city is a problem?"

FIGURE 5-3 You may have to travel to the respondent to conduct an interview. It's always wise to take notes and use a recording device.

The questions above are all *open-ended questions*, because they allow the respondent to elaborate on the answer. (We look at *closed-ended questions* in the section on surveys.) As you can see from these few examples, writing with precision is a must when designing interview questions.

Beyond your list of questions, you should think about where and how you will conduct the interviews. Will your questions be asked through email or in an online chat room or by telephone or face-to-face? There are advantages and disadvantages to each approach. *Email interviews* are impersonal, and do not allow for immediate follow-up questions. However, email is convenient for many people, and the digital format makes data collection and analysis an easy process. *Telephone interviews* are among the fastest ways to gather information, and they allow the interviewer to have some personal contact with the participant. This approach is especially helpful when a potential interviewee does not have time to meet in person. The disadvantages include developing an accurate and representative list of phone numbers (many people have unlisted numbers or cellphones, or some numbers may be for fax only), and people often consider unsolicited phone calls an intrusion. *In-person interviews* may be costly and slow, particularly if multiple interviewers are required. However, this form of interview enables maximum interaction between the respondent and the interviewer.

In addition to interviews, public relations professionals often conduct *focus groups*, which yield qualitative data. Focus groups are helpful for evaluating both inputs and outputs as shown in Macnamara's Pyramid.

Focus Groups. Focus groups typically consist of 8–12 people who represent the characteristics of your identified audience. Here, a trained facilitator leads a discussion and asks prepared questions to elicit opinions and experiences on specific topics. A successful focus group depends on being well organized and controlled. The facilitator should be armed with a list of clear, specific questions, beginning with some "get acquainted" warm-up questions that relax the group members and lead into the topic at hand, and then moving to more detailed, topical questions.

Focus groups tend to have two inherent problems. The first is attendance. The wise researcher will schedule the sessions to meet the needs of participants and will provide incentives to attract them. Both your budget and your participants will dictate the nature of an incentive. If your target public is college students, free pizza might suffice, but more sophisticated or affluent audiences may require monetary incentives to attend. It's also a good idea to overbook by one or two people to compensate for potential no-shows. The second problem is participation. It's not unusual to have one or two individuals who dominate the discussion and others who barely say a word. However, a well-trained facilitator should be able to guide the discussion and draw out the quieter participants.

It's a good idea to observe the focus group, and some professional facilities have viewing areas adjacent to focus group rooms for this purpose, as well as audio and video recorders. Be sure to watch the time carefully and conclude the session as scheduled, then thank and reward the participants. Once the session has concluded, review the data carefully to determine the answer(s) to your research question(s) and draft your report.

Quantitative Research Methods

There are three kinds of lies: lies, damn lies, and statistics.

~Origin Unknown.
Popularized by Mark Twain and often attributed to Benjamin Disraeli.

Two widely used quantitative methods in public relations are *content analyses* and *surveys*. The first looks at communication artifacts, such as news articles, speeches, books, brochures—anything that has been recorded in some way. The second asks people about their opinions, beliefs, attitudes, demographics, and preferences.

Content analysis. Although content analysis can be either qualitative or quantitative, it typically involves counting pre-defined words or phrases, so we consider it quantitative for our purposes. According to Babbie (2010), content analysis is "particularly well suited to … answering the classic question of communications research: 'Who says what, to whom, why, how, and with what effect?'" (p. 333). For example, you may want to analyze the texts of Web-based consumer reviews of your client's services to get a feel for what customers are saying. Perhaps you would count the number of times the words "recommend" and "not recommend" occur throughout all comments.

There are several advantages to using content analytic techniques. They tend to be economical and time efficient and can study processes and opinions over time (for instance, statements made during the last two years). However, content analysis is limited to recorded communications and is, therefore, not always comprehensive. One of the best ways to find out what people think is to ask them. That is often done through surveys.

Survey research. Survey research is one of the most widely used forms of research in public relations. It's therefore worth considering how to construct clear and valid survey instruments. Entire books have been written on the subject, but an overview of four types of questionnaire items is useful.

1. *Closed-ended* questions confine the respondent's answers in some way. Questions that can be answered with only a "yes" or a "no" are closed-ended. However, there are variations in survey instruments. Some *closed-ended questions* provide specific options. In an online questionnaire, the possible responses would appear as radio buttons, where only one choice can be selected. Here is an example of a *closed-ended question*:

Who would you like to see elected president?
- ❑ George Washington
- ❑ John Adams
- ❑ Herbert Hoover
- ❑ Woodrow Wilson
- ❑ Dwight Eisenhower

2. A *partially-closed* question allows the respondent to add a choice beyond those listed:

Who would you like to see elected president?
- ❑ George Washington
- ❑ John Adams
- ❑ Herbert Hoover
- ❑ Woodrow Wilson
- ❑ Dwight Eisenhower
- ❑ Other (specify): _____

3. *Rating scale* questions ask respondents to rate or rank their choices. The five-point *Likert Scale* is the basis for many of these assessments. (Pronounced LICK-ert, this scale is named after its developer, Rensis Lickert.) Likert items would be presented online with single-choice radio buttons. Here is an example of a Likert item:

State the degree to which you agree or disagree with the following statement.

I would like to see George Washington elected president.
- ○ Strongly disagree
- ○ Disagree
- ○ Neither agree nor disagree
- ○ Agree
- ○ Strongly agree

Semantic differential scales are difficult to write, because they must use precise antonyms, which are sometimes problematic. An online semantic differential item would use radio buttons that allow one response per set of opposites. An example of a semantic differential item might be:

How would you characterize Millard Fillmore as president?

Good	Bad
Weak	Strong
Decisive	Indecisive

A *balanced scale* questionnaire item offers the same number of answer options on either side of a midpoint and each option carries equal weight. Online responses are limited to one choice by the use of radio buttons. For example:

How satisfied are you with Calvin Coolidge's performance as president?
- ○ Very satisfied
- ○ Satisfied
- ○ Neither satisfied nor dissatisfied
- ○ Dissatisfied
- ○ Very dissatisfied

Unbalanced scales create biased data, because the answer options are skewed in one direction (such as eliminating the "very dissatisfied" option) and should be used with extreme caution.

4. *Open-ended* questions produce qualitative data. They are intended to encourage respondents to provide their own information, which can result in deeper understandings of the survey results. An online questionnaire would use a text box in which respondents can type several sentences or more. An example of an open-ended question is:

Who would you like to see elected president?

When constructing a questionnaire, consider how it will be administered (phone, Web, email, face-to-face, etc.) and how the data will be analyzed. Also think carefully about the format and the flow of questions. For example, it's wise to put demographic questions that may be viewed as sensitive last. That way, if a respondent abandons the questionnaire, you will not have lost all the data for that individual.

Sometimes, both qualitative and quantitative methods are used to provide a more complete picture of the topic at hand. Reflecting back on our lawn analogy, both counting the weeds per square foot and coring thoughtfully selected areas provide better information than either technique alone. The answers from both quantitative and qualitative research form the basis for deciding on an effective lawn treatment. This method of using qualitative and quantitative data in a single study is known as *triangulation*. No matter what methods are chosen, you must be able to explain the research methodologies you used to develop your public relations plan and how you plan to use research in your proposed program.

Writing the Research Section of the PR Plan

The decisions you make to develop the strategies, tactics, and tools in your public relations plan or proposal should be based on your research and the resulting situation analysis. It is important that you demonstrate to your client how you arrived at your conclusions.

Recall Petty and Caciappo's Elaboration Likelihood Model from Chapter 4. In a public relations proposal, you're using the *central route* to persuade a decision maker that your plan is sound, and your evidence is rock-solid research. There are many options for solving any public relations issue, and the burden is on you to show that you have developed a viable and effective plan. You therefore need to include in your plan both the facts that shaped your strategic decisions *and* where you found that information. In other words, you are offering a well-supported rationale for every strategic choice you have made.

The decisions you make to develop the strategies, tactics, and tools in your public relations plan or proposal should be based on your research and the resulting situation analysis.

Reporting secondary research is straightforward. You relate the information and cite your sources. However, primary research is more complex. You must describe the details of your methodology, your results, and their implications for the client and for the program plan. At the least, you should include the following information:

- Your sampling method and how many individuals were in the sample.

- How many individuals actually participated in the study (the "response rate").

- Why and how your research tools were developed. If you used a pre-designed questionnaire, describe the source, its reliability, and why it was chosen. If you designed your own survey instrument, you should include information on (1) what information the summary was designed to elicit, (2) how and why the questionnaire items were constructed, and (3) example items, as well as a sample of the full instrument in the appendix of the proposal.

- Results.

- Possible limitations of the research.

- How the research results informed the strategies, tactics, and tools proposed in the plan.

Once you have conducted adequate research to develop a situation analysis and the problem statement, you are ready to develop goals and objectives. We address these in Chapter 6.

Tying it All Together

Research is the foundation on which an entire public relations program is based. Both secondary and primary research can help you develop a meaningful and accurate situation analysis that will guide you to the problem statement. You collect and analyze data for primary research. Secondary research is information that others have produced, which you retrieve from a variety of online and offline sources. All research should be reported in the plan to demonstrate that sound decisions will lead to an effective public relations program.

Name _____Date _____

REFLECT AND REVIEW

1. Reflect on your own workplace or school. If you were to take a random sample of the population, how might you go about it?

   _____

   _____

   _____

   _____

2. Do a little online research about the Keeshond. Do you see any similarities between websites? How do they measure up in terms of the CARS Checklist? Which resource would you consider to have the highest quality? Why?

   _____

   _____

   _____

   _____

3. You want to know people's opinions of a new moisturizing skin cream. Write a balanced scale item for it.

   Very satisfied

   partially satisfied

   satisfied

   a diss appointed

   under satisfied

4. Try your hand at writing a Likert item for the same skin cream.

_____

_____

_____

_____

_____

CHAPTER 5 REFERENCES AND RESOURCES

Babbie, E. R. (2010). *The practice of social research*. Belmont, CA: Wadsworth.

Harris, R. D. (2012). *The CARS Checklist for information quality*. Retrieved from http://www.virtualsalt.com/evalu8it.htm

Macnamara, J. (2002). Research and evaluation. In C. Tymson & P. Lazar, *The New Australian and New Zealand Public Relations Manual* (pp. 100–134). Sydney: Tymson Communications.

Macnamara, J. R. (2011, December 9). PR metrics. *Whitepaper for the International Association for the Measurement and Evaluation of Communication*. Retrieved from http://amecorg.com/wp-content/uploads/2011/10/PR-Metrics-Paper.pdf

Rector, L. H. (2008). Comparison of Wikipedia and other encyclopedias for accuracy, breadth, and depth in historical articles. *Reference Services Review, 36*(1), 7–22.

Tolkien, J. R. R. (1937). *The Hobbit*. London: Allen & Unwin.

Watson, T., & Noble, P. (2007). *Evaluating public relations: A best practice guide to public relations planning, research and evaluation*. Philadelphia: Kogan Page.

Chapter 6
Writing the Public Relations
Plan: Step 2 Planning

© 2012 by Miguel Angel
Salina Salinas. Used under
license of Shutterstock, Inc.

*A vision without a plan is just a dream. A plan without a vision is just
drudgery. But a vision with a plan can change the world.*

~ Old Proverb, Origin Unknown

This chapter adopts a Management by Objectives approach and describes the criteria
for developing and writing effective goals and objectives. It draws connections between
well-written objectives and program management tools, including calendar, budget, and
program evaluation techniques. It also expands on audience analysis from Chapter 5
to describe primary and secondary publics and develop key messages for each target.

LEARNING OBJECTIVES:

The information presented in this chapter will enable you to:

1. Identify and establish a clear public relations goal, based
   on the client's goals and the problem statement developed
   from a situation analysis.

2. Write clear, measurable, actionable objectives that support
   the stated goals.

3. Develop effective key messages for target publics.

4. Create a systematic and thorough public relations plan.

Once you have done extensive research, analyzed the data, and developed a situation analysis and problem statement, it's time to develop the *goals* and *objectives* for your public relations program plan. In other words, in Step 1, you asked and answered your formative research questions, and now, in Step 2, you establish your target outcomes. One way to do that is to use the PR Management by Objectives (PR-MBO) approach, which was initially proposed in 1984 by Professors Norman Nager and Thomas Allen.

First popularized by Peter Drucker in 1954, Management by Objectives (MBO) was intended to involve organizational employees in setting their own goals, which increases motivation and commitment. Establishing measurable goals also provides managers with measurable criteria by which to evaluate employee performance. Although the concept has its detractors, MBO is still used in organizations today, and it is invaluable for the practice of public relations.

PR-MBO establishes goals and objectives that describe measurable public relations program outcomes. Remember that program outcomes constitute the top level of Macnamara's Pyramid Model in Chapter 5. Those outcomes demonstrate to decision makers that your program is yielding a reasonable return on investment (ROI). By writing clear goals and measurable objectives, you are developing the basis for measuring program outcomes and ROI. Furthermore, because well-written objectives specify what is to be accomplished and by when, they will lead you to appropriate measurement tools. The first step is identifying your public relations goals.

Establishing and Writing Goals and Objectives

Goals are accomplishments that are to be realized at some point in the future. They define an organization's general aims and need not be measurable nor have target dates, although they sometimes do.

Writing Public Relations Goals

The nature of your public relations plan will depend on your client's goals. Long-term organizational goals may be five years or more in the future. Short-term goals, as the name implies, are to be realized much sooner. If the client has a long-term vision or strategic plan, it will undoubtedly contain long-term goals that will guide you as you establish your public relations goals and objectives. (There's that secondary research again!) A Request for Proposals (RFP) also typically includes specific goals that the client hopes to achieve in the short term.

In a 2009 whitepaper published by the Institute for Public Relations, Forrest W. Anderson, Linda Hadley, David Rockland, and Mark Weiner listed some general categories of business goals (p. 7):

- *"Increasing business performance*, often measured in terms of sales, market share, stock price, earnings per share, etc.

- *"Optimizing the use of labor and capital*, for example through increased productivity, greater efficiency, or employee retention

- *"Avoiding catastrophic loss* by, for example, mitigating a crisis, averting calamitous reputation damage, or protecting market capitalization"

Most of the time, your client will have organizational goals that fit into one or more of these areas. Your job, then, is to develop public relations goals that translate the client's goals into actionable and measurable outcomes. In addition, public relations research sometimes identifies problems or opportunities that your client should act on. In both cases, you need, first, to develop public relations goals and, second, write measurable objectives to attain those goals. As you write your plan, bear in mind that each section builds on the last. Therefore, the *goals you establish for your plan must*:

1. *support the client's stated goals, and*

2. *directly address the issue(s) you identified in your problem statement.*

Let's consider a hypothetical situation in which economic downturns have led to restructuring and layoffs in an organization. Both employee morale and productivity have declined. The company's business goal, then, might be stated: "to increase productivity." After doing some research for your situation analysis, you find that productivity is often linked to employee morale. You also learn through primary research that company employees are concerned about job security, and that they perceive little

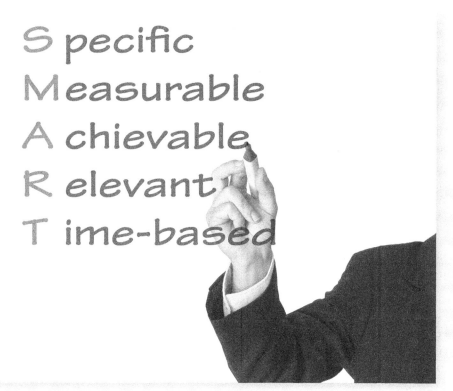

FIGURE 6-1
One way to remember the characteristics of well-written objectives is with the acronym SMART.

communication from management beyond a monthly employee newsletter. Your situation analysis, therefore, has led to a problem statement that identifies employee morale and productivity as being connected to a "widespread concern that the company lacks transparency." As a result, it would be reasonable to establish a public relations goal "to improve internal communications." One outcome objective, therefore, might be "to improve employee perceptions of transparency by 10 percent by the end of the year." The specific ways in which you plan to accomplish this objective will constitute your *tactics*.

Writing Public Relations Objectives

Writing clear, measurable objectives takes considerable thought and practice. Dr. George T. Doran developed some useful guidelines for writing clear objectives, using the acronym S.M.A.R.T. (1981). His acronym has been modified over the years with a variety of meanings. For our public relations purposes, we use it to represent *Specific, Measurable, Achievable, Relevant, and Time-based*. Let's examine each of those characteristics.

Objectives Should Be *Specific*. To be effective, each objective should specify (1) the public(s) to which it is targeted, (2) the date by which it will be accomplished, (3) how it will be attained, and the (4) method by which it will be measured. A well-written objective enables you to demonstrate the value of your results. That sounds like quite a mouthful, and it is. Careful writing and economy of words is a "must." The IPR whitepaper by Anderson et al. lists six examples of well-written public relations objectives (p. 12). Each example of an objective in the bulleted items below identifies a target public, which is noted here by boxed text:

1. "Impressions: Create 10 million impressions through 200 placements in national print and broadcast outlets that mention study findings by the end of the campaign in June.

2. "Reach: By the end of the second fiscal quarter in June 2009, reach 35% of registered dietitians and nutrition professors with "leadership" messages through placements in top 20 target markets.

3. "Comprehension: Create an understanding of insurance pricing models among 75% of insured adults by the end of the campaign in November.

4. "Awareness: Raise awareness of "cleaning power" among women 25–34 from 20% last year to 50% this year.

5. "Attitude: By the end of the year, convince 10% of customers that bank fees are an acceptable charge.

6. "Behavior: Between this year and next, increase from 15% to 25% the percent of insured customers who recommend our brand to their friends or family."

Each of these objectives is well focused and specific, using precise language. We revisit them in the following sections to illustrate various characteristics of objectives.

Objectives Should Be *Measurable*. Well-written objectives *operationalize* the results you plan to achieve. Incorporating quantities, frequencies, and quality adds measurability to written objectives:

- *Quantities and Frequencies*: Counting numbers of votes cast or media impressions or units sold or numbers of press clippings are all examples of quantities. Frequencies are quantities over time, such as how many times per hour a museum exhibit is visited. Note the quantity in the example from the IPR whitepaper list of objectives:

  1. "Impressions: Create 10 million impressions through 200 placements in national print and broadcast outlets that mention study findings by the end of the campaign in June."

- *Quality*: Achieving a given standard may be written as numbers, while improvements over a previous standard or objective might be expressed as a percentage.

  4. "Awareness: Raise awareness of "cleaning power" among women 25–34 from 20% last year to 50% this year."

We address some specific measurement tools in Chapter 8. For now, we look at additional characteristics of well-written objectives.

Objectives Should Be *Achievable*. Any objective must be reasonable and attainable. As with all steps of the public relations process, you may need to do some additional research to determine the achievability of an objective. Do you have enough time? Is the budget adequate? Are decision makers likely to agree with your analyses and conclusions? Are you overreaching a norm? Do environmental influences interfere with the plan? You need answers to these and other questions to be sure your objectives are achievable.

Objectives Should Be *Relevant*. No matter how noble or inspired your objectives may be, if they are not relevant to the client's stated goals and desired outcomes, they are useless. Be sure to review your objectives to verify that (1) they directly support the client's goals and (2) the client agrees with your assessment.

Objectives Should Be *Time-Based*. Every objective you write should have a target date by which it will be attained. Beginners often make the mistake of including such phrases as "each week" or "daily" or "every month." These are not target dates, because they are ongoing periods of time. They are fine for describing standing plans, but not for objectives. A well-written objective includes a *specific point in time* when it is to be accomplished, such as "July 1" or "by the end of the campaign," or "at the end of the third quarter." Note the concrete target dates in IPR Whitepaper objectives below:

1. "Impressions: Create 10 million impressions through 200 placements in national print and broadcast outlets that mention study findings by the end of the campaign in June,

2. "Reach: By the end of the second fiscal quarter in June 2009, reach 35% of registered dietitians and nutrition professors with "leadership" messages through placements in top 20 target markets.

3. "Comprehension: Create an understanding of insurance pricing models among 75% of insured adults by the end of the campaign in November.

5. "Attitude: By the end of the year, convince 10% of customers that bank fees are an acceptable charge."

Be sure to set reasonable target dates. Build in as much room as possible for media lead times, client approvals and revisions, and unforeseen delays.

Levels of Objectives. Referring again to Macnamara's Pyramid Model of PR Research from Chapter 5, consider the three levels of Input, Output, and Outcomes as three levels of public relations objectives. The way in which any objective is measured depends on the level of that objective:

FIGURE 6-2
When presented together, well-written objectives, like a pilot's flight plan, spell out where you are going, as well as a timeline and benchmarks along the way.

© 2012 by Al_Kan . Used under license of Shutterstock, Inc.

- *Input* is the foundational level of the Pyramid, which we might expand to include *production objectives*. Objectives at this level are measured with such methods as tracking the number of materials produced, contacts made, etc. Research for this level includes such techniques as readability indexes or message testing.

- *Output* objectives include campaign processes, which are evaluated by such measures as the number of messages sent, audience comprehension, message retention, etc.

- *Outcomes* objectives are measured by changes in audience attitudes, opinions, awareness, or behaviors.

Although you begin formative research at the bottom of the Pyramid, as you begin writing your objectives, you should focus on the top. Here, you state precisely what your public relations program outcomes and impacts will be in measurable terms. Objectives for the middle and bottom levels of the Pyramid, program output and program input, describe how you plan to accomplish those outcomes. Three of the Anderson et al. objectives are Outcomes objectives and include measurements of *awareness*, *attitudes*, and *behavior*:

4. "Awareness: Raise awareness of "cleaning power" among women 25–34 from 20% last year to 50% this year.

5. "Attitude: By the end of the year, convince 10% of customers that bank fees are an acceptable charge.

6. "Behavior: Between this year and next, increase from 15% to 25% the percent of insured customers who recommend our brand to their friends or family."

The other three objectives are Output objectives, with measurements of *comprehension*, *impressions*, and *reach*.[1]

1. "Impressions: Create 10 million impressions through 200 placements in national print and broadcast outlets that mention study findings by the end of the campaign in June.

2. "Reach: By the end of the second fiscal quarter in June 2009, reach 35% of registered dietitians and nutrition professors with "leadership" messages through placements in top 20 target markets.

3. "Comprehension: Create an understanding of insurance pricing models among 75% of insured adults by the end of the campaign in November."

Keep in mind that all your PR outcomes and impacts should directly affect the client's ROI, and that your objectives must demonstrate that aim.

Linking PR Objectives with the ROI. In addition to Output and Outcome objectives, the Anderson et al. whitepaper notes that you should establish at least one objective for *business results*. If you have done a thorough and well-researched situation analysis, identified an appropriate problem statement, and taken care to directly respond to the client's stated business goals with supporting public relations goals and objectives, establishing business results should be a straightforward process.

---

[1] Anderson, Hadley, Rockland, and Weiner (2009) classify "comprehension" as an outcome objective; however, this text uses Macnamara's Pyramid of PR Research, in which comprehension is an output.

FIGURE 6-3
Measurable objectives help determine the tools you will use to determine program effectiveness.

Returning to our hypothetical case of increasing employee morale by improving internal communications, recall that we established a goal of improving employee morale, as well as a public relations Outcome objective "to improve employee perceptions of transparency by 10 percent by the end of the year." The supporting business result or ROI objective might be "to increase employee productivity by 3 percent or $21,000 of salable product through improved morale by the end of the year."

So far, we have looked only at Output, Outcome, and Business objectives that either deal with program processes or outcomes. Inputs or "production objectives" have purposely been set aside for separate discussion because they require special attention.

Production Is not Necessarily an Objective. One mistake to avoid is that of developing objectives at the level of public relations tools. Be sure to maintain focus on program outcomes and outputs. Writing press releases or holding an event or producing a brochure may well help you realize your objectives, and you certainly will report such productivity. However, activities do not need to be written as objectives in their own right, and we address how to describe activities, tools, and tactics in Chapter 7. That said, writing solid Input or production objectives, *when used to support your Output, Outcome, and Business objectives*, are helpful for establishing your timeline and budget.

Input objectives help you develop important elements of your plan, because they provide such things as target dates and possibly even costs for your plan's timeline and budget. For example, you might write an Input objective to "produce and distribute 5,000 bi-fold brochures to consumers by December 7 at a cost not to exceed $2,000." Note that the distribution day provides a target date that you can incorporate into your timeline (brochures distributed by December 7), as well as a line item for your budget (5,000 brochures at $2,000).

Identifying PR Goals and Objectives

Establishing the client's goal as it relates to a public relations program sometimes requires a little diagnostic work. For example, a small mom-and-pop client may state that its goal is a newsletter. Clearly, a newsletter is a tool and not a goal. Therefore, your job is to determine what the goal really is. Professors Nager and Allen, in their book on PR-MBO, provided a simple diagnostic tool in the form of two questions: "Why?" and "How?" In this case, if you ask the client why a newsletter is wanted, you will eventually unearth what the client hopes to accomplish. As noted at the beginning of this chapter, the client's goal likely is related to increasing organizational performance, optimizing resources, or avoiding loss. Similarly, if you know the client's goal, you can identify your public relations objectives by asking "how?" This helps ensure that the goals and objectives you establish appropriately support the client's stated goals.

Once you have written your goals and objectives, you have expressed what you want to accomplish in measurable terms, by when, and for what audience. Your next step, then, is to develop the messages for each audience that will best achieve those aims.

Developing the Key Messages

In Chapter 5, we explored research methods by which to identify and describe your target publics. In this chapter, we revisit that information to determine primary and secondary publics, as well as develop effective key messages for them.

Understanding Primary and Secondary Publics

Primary publics are comprised of the people you are trying to influence. These are the individuals you hope to persuade to buy a product, vote a particular way, fasten their seatbelts, or think of the client in positive terms. For our purposes, *secondary publics* are groups or individuals who can influence primary publics in some way. The most obvious examples of secondary publics are the media, but secondary publics also include the *influencers* you identified through your research and audience analysis.

Once you have made research-based decisions to identify and develop comprehensive psychographic and demographic profiles of the primary and secondary target publics, you need to write a key message for each. Consistent messages ensure cohesiveness throughout all of your program materials. *Everything you plan to do throughout the program should be designed to convey the key messages you craft at this stage of the plan.* Remember that you must consider audience motivations, values, lifestyles, and in the case of media, newsworthiness to develop meaningful key messages.

Key Messages Are Not Tag Lines

Developing key messages is really a matter of considering what your client wants to communicate to key publics. It does not have to be cute or catchy—that can come later. What you are developing at this point is the content of the communication, not the packaging.

The well-written key message has two components. The first is a single, declarative sentence that describes a core idea you want to convey. If your target public remembers nothing else, this is the one thing you want it to know. The second is a short list (no more than three or four items) of supporting information. Again, these statements should be simple, declarative sentences. The Texas Commission on the Arts (TCA, n.d.), in its online Tool-Kit, provides a pocket-sized card of four key messages. Each is simple, easy to understand, and states a core idea accompanied by bullet points to enhance or expand on the core idea. The first message broadly addresses the role of art in people's lives:

"Art is everywhere."

- "Art encourages thought and reason, imagination and creativity. Art inspires. Art communicates. Art opens eyes, opens hearts and opens doors."

- "Art and culture permeate our lives through individual and collective expression and experiences."

- "Imagine what your life or your community would be like without art."

The other key messages focus on the importance of the Commission and its fundraising efforts. Note that the following key message is clearly targeted to a specific key public:

"TCA unites the arts community of Texas."

- "TCA supports the visual, performing, folk, literary and multimedia arts that significantly contribute to the state's educational, economic and cultural future."

- "In order to support the arts in Texas, TCA needs the support of each of our constituents, the state legislature and private contributors."

The TCA key messages provide an excellent example of an important principle in nonprofit public relations. Whether targeting donors or consumers, it is imperative that the importance of the mission is emphasized, as well as the importance of funding that mission.

Use a Planning Checklist

As you move through this step of writing your public relations plan and into the next step of implementation, verify that you are being systematic and thorough with the following checklist:

- Have you established a clear *public relations goal* that supports the client's business goal?

- Do you have specific, measurable, attainable, relevant, and time-based *objectives*?

- Did your research lead you to identify and thoroughly describe the values, attitudes, and lifestyles of appropriate primary and secondary *target publics*?

- Have you developed meaningful *key messages* for your target publics?

- Have you translated your key messages into a memorable or inspiring *campaign identification* (your "Big Idea")?

- What *strategies*, *tools*, and *tactics* will you use to convey your key messages to the target publics? You need to develop these in the Implementation section of your public relations plan, which is described in Chapter 7.

OneVoice and Philips Norelco (2011) developed a campaign for the Philips Norelco BG 2040 bodygrooming product that demonstrates the effectiveness of careful planning and articulating each of these checklist items:

- Several *goals* were established, including a business goal to boost sales of the BG 2040 Bodygroom.

- The public relations *objectives* included rebuilding awareness in Norelco Bodygroomers and developing in the target public an understanding of the benefits of purchasing the BG 2040.

- The *target public* comprised men aged 25–50. Research indicated that 87% of men in this demographic considered preserving the environment as being important and that 64% of Millennials, which include the younger members of the target demographic, would be willing to pay more for a product that also offered an investment in an environmental cause.

- The *key message* was introducing the new BG 2040 and the brand "Philips Norelco" or "Norelco" with a link to environmental reforestation. Norelco promised to plant a tree for every Bodygroom sold.

- The key message was translated into a *campaign ID* of "Deforest Yourself, Reforest the World."

- The campaign *strategy* was one of providing men "a new and compelling reason to learn about grooming, talk about it, and be inspired by it," and it included a celebrity spokesperson who would appeal to the target public. This led to a launch on Arbor Day with Carmen Electra grooming hairy men in New York. Other *tools* and *tactics* included integrated communications, media outreach, and online engagement through the pre-existing www.shaveeverywhere.com website.

The results of the campaign were excellent. The program successfully engaged the target public, and Norelco donated $75,000 (75,000 trees) to the Arbor Day Foundation. BG 2040 product sales increased by a whopping 18% at program launch, and OneVoice and Philips Norelco won a 2011 PRSA Silver Anvil Award for the "Deforest Yourself, Reforest the World" public relations campaign.

Tying It All Together

The planning section of a public relations plan involves identifying the client's business goals and then establishing public relations goals and objectives that will help achieve them. Objectives must be specific, measurable, and include target dates, but goals can be more general. PR goals and objectives should link back to the client's organizational goals.

Public relations professionals should craft succinct key messages for each audience that was identified during the research phase of the PR process, keeping in mind all goals and objectives. Well-written messages are simple declarative statements that represent the key concepts to be conveyed throughout the entire program. A solid plan includes (1) goals, (2) objectives, (3) full, research-based profiles of target publics, (4) key messages for those publics, (5) a memorable and unifying campaign identification that is based on the key messages, and (6) strategies, tools, and tactics to convey your key messages to the target publics.

Name _____ Date _____

REFLECT AND REVIEW

1. Write one meaningful, personal goal.

   _____

   _____

   _____

2. Write three *specific*, *measurable*, and *time-bound* objectives that will directly help you attain the goal you wrote above. **Caution:** Avoid anything ongoing, such as monthly bank deposits, daily calorie counts, completing weekly assignments, etc.

   a. _____

   b. _____

   c. _____

3. Reflect on your place of employment or school. What is its primary organizational goal? (Example: The goal of the American Cancer Society is to eradicate cancer.)

   _____

   _____

4. Based on the organizational goal you identified above, write one key message.

   _____

   _____

   _____

   _____

   _____

CHAPTER 6 REFERENCES AND RESOURCES

Anderson, F. W., Hadley, L., Rockland, D., & Weiner, M. (2009). *Guidelines for setting measurable public relations objectives: An update* [Whitepaper]. Gainesville, FL: The Institute for Public Relations, Commission on PR Measurement and Evaluation. Retrieved from http://www.instituteforpr.org/wp-content/uploads/Setting_PR_Objectives.pdf

Doran, G. T. (1981). There's a S.M.A.R.T. way to write management's goals and objectives. *Management Review, 70*(11), 35–36.

Drucker, P. F. (1954). *The practice of management.* New York: HarperCollins.

Nager, N. R., & Allen, T. H. (1984). *Public relations management by objectives.* New York: Longman.

OneVoice & Philips Norelco. (2011). *Philips Norelco Deforest Yourself, Reforest the World.* Retrieved from http://www.prsa.org/SearchResults/view/6BW-1103A32/0/Philips_Norelco_Deforest_Yourself_Reforest_the_Wor

Texas Commission on the Arts. (n.d.). *Tool-kit.* Austin: Author. Retrieved from http://www.arts.state.tx.us/toolkit/advocacy/templates/key.pdf

Chapter 7

Writing the Public Relations Plan: Step 3 Implementation

© 2012 by Ilin Sergey.
Used under license of
Shutterstock, Inc.

It is not always what we know or analyzed before we make a decision that makes it a great decision. It is what we do after we make the decision to implement and execute it that makes it a good decision.

~William Pollard

This chapter explains how the communication or execution phase of a public relations program should be described in a PR plan, including appropriate content and format for effective and accurate calendars and budgets.

LEARNING OBJECTIVES

The information presented in this chapter will enable you to:

1. Incorporate strategic approaches into a public relations plan.

2. Determine appropriate tactics and tools to convey key messages to target publics.

3. Develop a public relations program calendar and present it in the form of a Gantt chart.

4. Design a realistic operating budget for a public relations program.

So far, your plan has identified a problem statement, established your program goals and objectives, defined and established psychographic profiles of the target publics, and articulated the key messages you plan to send to those publics. This section of the plan explains in detail how you will convey your key messages to the target publics.

One mistake to avoid when writing a plan is the overuse of bullet points. Although they are helpful to provide overviews or summaries or bring the reader's eye to key ideas, bullet points tend to result in a lack of detail. It is critical to write out every feature of your plan. *If it isn't in the written document, it doesn't exist for the client.*

Defining and Describing the Strategies

Chapter 4 described ways to use creativity and Big Ideas to develop strategies, and Chapter 6 explained that those ideas should be consistent with your key messages. The Implementation section of your plan should explain your strategies. Organize this section of the plan according to your target publics, with an introductory paragraph that explains and justifies the overall strategic approach you have chosen. Then the plan should outline the strategy with which you will engage each of your target publics, as well as describe why you chose that particular approach. In addition, this section should specify your overarching strategy for the entire program.

The strategies you develop will depend on the information you have gathered and analyzed thus far, especially your target audience profiles. By focusing on audience, you can determine the strategies that will be most effective to convey your key messages. Do not expect the target public to come to you. Determine what reaches your audience and go there. What theme will you use to unify all components of your plan? What emotional appeals will work for each targeted psychographic profile? Examine your goals and objectives, as well as the nature of your target publics, to develop effective strategies. A U.S. Centers for Disease Control and Prevention (CDC) campaign (2011) for emergency preparedness provides a good illustration of this idea.

FIGURE 7-1.
The U.S. Centers for Disease Control and Prevention used a strategy that capitalized on the popularity of zombie lore to encourage emergency preparedness.

U.S. Centers for Disease Control and Prevention

In 2010, the CDC launched a well-thought-out public education campaign with a strategy intended to appeal to a very broad American audience, including youth. The campaign, "Preparedness 101: Zombie Apocalypse," won a 2011 *PRNews* Platinum PR Award. The program strategy capitalized on the popularity of zombie stories. It described the history of zombies in the U.S. culture and how to prepare for a potential "Zombie Apocalypse." It then provided extensive information on emergency preparedness. The key message, which was to plan and prepare for potential emergencies, was evident in all materials. The CDC tactics were well suited to the target demographic and included social media such as blogs, RSS feeds, Twitter, and Facebook. "Zombie Task Force" t-shirts were available for purchase through the CDC Foundation, and a graphic novel presented emergency preparedness in a unique way.

Beyond the News Release: Selecting Effective Tactics and Tools

The introduction to this text defines tactics as the general communication modes you choose to reach your target publics. In other words, you are looking at the *types* of channels through which you will send your key messages. Examples of public relations tactics are print or broadcast or social media, in-person meetings, calendars, collateral materials, and many more. In fact, the tactics you can employ are as limitless as your target publics. You just won't have enough time or money to implement them all. That's why it's important to give serious thought to the tactics that your research indicates you should use to reach each of your target publics.

Be sure you know what (or if) each target public reads, what it listens to, what it watches, its leisure activities, its cultural norms, and how information flows within its communities.

Select Appropriate Tactics. Not every tactic works for every public. For example, if you were targeting a low-income population whose first language is not English, social media would be a poor choice. This demographic group is unlikely to have either the access or the expertise to receive messages through online means. On the other hand, a broadly defined population that includes a young demographic, such as the one in the CDC example above, is an excellent target to approach through social media.

As always, a thorough, well-researched audience analysis is your key to successfully determining appropriate tactics. Do not assume anything. Be sure you know what (or if) each target public reads, what it listens to, what it watches, its leisure activities, its cultural norms, and how information flows within its communities. Your best channel might be a grassroots approach, working with informal community leaders and face-to-face conversations, or it might be a popular leisure activity.

Hill and Knowlton and Johnson & Johnson won the PRSA 2011 Best of Silver Anvil Award with their *text4baby* program (2011), in part because their research-based tactics were so effective in reaching the target demographics. The free mobile information service was designed to promote maternal and child health. *Text4baby's* success was due to a broad public-private partnership, including the National Healthy Mothers, Healthy Babies Coalition, Voxiva, and CTIA-The Wireless Foundation—among others—with Johnson & Johnson as the founding sponsor. Secondary audiences included mommy bloggers, health reporters, and a variety of federal, state, and local organizations. The PRSA summary reports that the "program helped build a network of 134,000 subscribers (and counting) and recruit 500+ partners to spread the word."

Although the program focused on a series of weekly texts, the campaign used many other tactics and tools, as well. One key public was African American women in the Southern states with limited incomes, because infant mortality rates were higher within this demographic. Such tactics as recruiting national, state, and community partners who worked directly with mothers and families, identifying an appropriate (and willing) celebrity spokesperson, and partnering with BET and American Urban Radio Networks all helped reach this target.

Select Appropriate Tools. Recall from the introduction to this text that tools are the specific elements of your tactics. For example, if a tactic is to use broadcast, the specific channels or networks you choose are your tools. In the award-winning *text-4baby* case described above, one tactic was to recruit Sherri Shepherd of *The View*, because she appealed to the younger African American audience and she had a son with health problems related to a premature birth. Similarly, MTV was approached as a media partner because the network was highly popular with teens, and teen mothers constituted another target demographic.

In addition, consider the best ways to distribute your information to both primary and secondary target publics. For example, news releases often extend far beyond traditional print and broadcast media. *Smart news releases* provide online content in multiple formats, including multimedia, and enable immediate download for a variety of media outlet platforms. *Social media news releases* provide online content specifically designed to encourage interactivity, such as blogs, RSS feeds, bookmarking, and the like.

Once you have described the strategies, tools, and tactics you propose to use, you must spell out the proposed timeline and budget in the implementation section of the plan. Timing and costs are critical factors for decision makers.

The Public Relations Program Timeline

If you have written specific, measurable, and time-bound objectives, you are already well on your way to determining the calendar schedule for your program. Your research will also tell you the best timing for your plan. For example, skin cancer education programs may be best launched when swimwear appears in the stores each spring.

Start your calendar with your program completion target date and work backward. Then plug in dates for your tactics and tools. As mentioned in Chapter 6, be sure to incorporate appropriate lead time as required by targeted media, as well as time for revisions and client approval processes. Include in your calendar evaluation requirements, such as pre-campaign benchmark surveys and postcampaign awareness surveys. Everything in your plan should appear in your schedule, and everything in your schedule must appear in your plan.

The best way to present a timeline in the public relations plan is as a Gantt chart. This is a visual representation of your full program schedule, including the start and completion of every tool and its preparation. First developed by Henry Gantt, this chart is a widely used standard in project planning because it allows you to see at a glance when each element of the plan is to be started and completed. Typically, the planned activities are listed down the left side, and the calendar is depicted horizontally across the top, as shown in Table 7-1.

TABLE 7-1: A Gantt chart visually displays every detail of a public relations calendar and provides an overview of all activities during a given period.

	Jan	Feb	Mar	Apr	May	Jun
Photography for Brochure	■					
News Releases Written		■	■	■	■	
News Release Approvals			■	■	■	
News Release Distributions				■	■	■
Mini-Seminars		■				
Brochure Writing		■	■			
Brochure Layout			■			
Brochure Revisions & Approvals				■	■	
Brochure Printing & Folding					■	■
Brochure Distribution						■

There are a number of software programs that will generate Gantt charts, but they can be developed as tables through word processing programs, such as Microsoft Word or Apple Pages or in spreadsheet software, such as Microsoft Excel or Apple Numbers. Gantt charts do have some limitations. They tend to become unwieldy if you have more than 30 activities, and you need to give serious thought to how the chart layout will graphically appear in your plan or proposal. You will probably need to use landscape orientation, if it fits on a single page, or you may need to print the chart on a long (11"x17") page that folds into the document. Whatever format you use, the Gantt chart must be readable and professional looking, and the color scheme and fonts should be consistent with the rest of the document. As you implement the plan, a blowup of your Gantt chart posted on a wall helps you stay on track.

While maintaining a program schedule is important, you also need to establish and stick to a realistic budget. Like everything else in your plan, you probably will need to do some research to determine the costs of your program elements.

The Public Relations Program Budget

The budget is a plan for spending. Exact formats and billing structures vary widely. For example, according to a whitepaper by J. Francisco Escobar (2008) for the Council of Public Relations Firms, a 2007 business benchmarking survey by the Council indicated that "nearly 45% of its member firms are engaged in time-based contracts," and another "34% use either a fixed fee or retainer basis for billing clients" (p. 3). If you are working within a firm, your employer probably will establish the mode of compensation for you. Bear in mind, though, that your final budget must incorporate such direct and indirect costs as overhead and team members' time.

The budget section of your PR plan should open with a descriptive paragraph or two that provides a budget overview and describes any possible reductions, such as printing in two colors or black-and-white instead of a four-color process. As always, provide your rationale for why the proposed expenditures are cost effective. Bear in mind that what you or the client want to do may differ from what is affordable. You

FIGURE 7-2. A public relations program must be realistic and find the intersection between what is desired and what is affordable, as well as how much time is available.

are trying to maximize ROI and do as much as possible within the client's financial limitations. Once implemented, your completed program will be evaluated, in part, on how well you stayed within budget.

In addition to the description, this section of the PR plan includes a table that outlines the specifics of the proposed budget. It must include every cost associated with each element you have proposed, right down to the last postage stamp. *Your budget cannot be too detailed.* Writing the budget section is a good opportunity to cross check that you have done a thorough job of describing your tactics and tools and scheduling them. Everything you list in the budget must be listed in your calendar *and* included in your descriptions of the strategies, tactics, and tools. Similarly, everything you have described in the plan and listed in the timeline must be covered in the budget.

Writing the budget section is a good opportunity to cross check that you have done a thorough job of describing your tactics and tools and of scheduling them on your timeline.

Professor Kirk Hallahan, APR, Fellow PRSA, of Colorado State University, offers on his website (2004) an excellent checklist of items to include in a budget:

Campaigns Budget Reminder Checklist

(Organized by spending category—also can be outlined by activity. Only include anticipated items.)

Staffing:

>   Salaries: Each staffer @ hourly rate based on salary.
>   Benefits (if paid by dept): Social Security, health plan, benefits = 30%+/-
>   Office Occupancy (if paid by dept): Rent, Furniture, Phone, Equipment, Non-chargeable supplies

Consultants/Professional Fees:

>   Includes freelancers/contract labor

Direct Program Costs:

Research:

>   Books
>   Subscriptions (dues and subscriptions)
>   On-line computer services
>   Other research purchased

Publicity:

>   Letterheads, press kits
>   Duplicating/lettershop
>   Mailing supplies/list charges
>   PR distribution services
>   Clipping/broadcast monitoring

Photography/Videography

>   Staff time
>   Film stock/digital media, processing
>   Model fees
>   Props
>   Rentals, other production expenses

Advertising:

>   Design fees/charges
>   Production/distribution
>   Time/space charges by media

Controlled Media:

>   Design
>   Publications printing
>   Distribution/fulfillment
>   Purchases: Advertising specialties

Interactive Media:

     Website Hosting/Internet Service Provider
     Webmastering services, design
     Site registration fees
     Software

Events:

     Promotion/tickets/name badges
     Venue/equipment rentals
     Catering/refreshments (include supplies)
     Entertainment/speaker expenses
     Staffing/security
     Communications expenses
     Prizes/giveaways

General: Distribution/Communication Expense:

     Postage
     Overnight delivery/freight
     Facsimile
     Photocopying/duplicating
     Cell phones
     Telephone services (long distance, including incoming 800 number, if any)

General: Travel & Entertainment:

     Airline/other public transit
     Mileage reimbursement for staff
     Meals
     Conference registrations for meetings

General: Equipment/Supply/Software purchases

Subtotal of above

Contingency Reserve: Add 10-15% to the above and subtotal as reserve

Grand Total

Courtesy of Kirk Hallahan, Colorado State University.

The content of your budget should conform to Professor Hallahan's outline above and spell out each element in detail. In addition, since public relations programs typically are implemented over time, it is helpful to show the weeks or months during which expenditures are anticipated. See Table 7-2 for an abbreviated example of a hypothetical public relations budget format.

Note that the budget and the calendar must match, and both should reflect your written objectives. Remember that you are writing a clear, cohesive, persuasive document with the intention of getting your proposed plan approved. Therefore, it is to your benefit to make the plan, including the calendar and budget, as clear and readable as possible.

TABLE 7-2. A partial public relations budget showing fictitious figures. Note that the monthly totals on the far right and the monthly subtotals in italics both add up to the same figure. The specifics of each line item, such as provider name or number of pieces should appear in the left column. All items, even those to be donated or underwritten, should be included in the preliminary budget.

Direct Program Costs	Jan	Feb	Mar	Apr	May	Jun	Totals
Research							
Books (specify titles)	$350						$350
Dues & Subscriptions (specify)	$200						$200
Focus Groups		$2,500					$2,500
Pre-Post Campaign Surveys	$1,250	$0	$0	$0	$0	$1,250	$2,500
Subtotal	*$1,800*	*$2,500*	*$0*	*$0*	*$0*	*$1,250*	*$5,550*
Publicity							
Press Kits	$0	$0	$1,275	$0	$0	$0	$1,275
Mailing Supplies & Postage	$0	$0	$1,200	$0	$0	$0	$1,200
Distribution Service (specify)	$0	$0	$800	$0	$0	$0	$800
Media Monitoring & Clipping Service	$0	$0	$700	$700	$700	$700	$2,800
Printing & Folding × 1,000	$0	$1,500	$0	$0	$0	$0	$1,500
Subtotal	*$0*	*$1,500*	*$3,975*	*$700*	*$700*	*$700*	*$7,575*
Program Total	*$1,800*	*$4,000*	*$3,975*	*$700*	*$700*	*$1,950*	*$13,125*

Tying It All Together

The implementation section of a public relations plan is much like the instructions in a recipe. Once the ingredients are listed, the instructions explain the order and method of combining them, the cooking time, and any special handling instructions. Similarly, a well-written public relations plan spells out your proposed strategies, tactics, and tools for each target public and explains exactly how and when you propose to carry them out. Graphic representations of the proposed schedule and budget help the client understand the time and costs involved in the plan. Therefore, the program elements and implementation dates must match in both the budget and the timeline.

Name _____ Date _____

REFLECT AND REVIEW

1. Reflect on the nature of your employer or university. Who are its key publics?

    _____

    _____

    _____

2. Keeping in mind one of the key publics you listed in #1 above, list at least three tactics that you believe would best reach them.

    _____

    _____

    _____

3. Based on one of the tactics you identified in #2, list three tools you would use to deliver your key messages.

    _____

    _____

    _____

4. For each of the following, mark the box that correctly identifies it as a strategy, tactic, or tool.

	Strategy	Tactic	Tool
The New York Times	❏	❏	❏
Being fashionable	❏	❏	❏
New releases	❏	❏	❏
MTV	❏	❏	❏
Social media	❏	❏	❏
Facebook	❏	❏	❏
Events	❏	❏	❏
Seasonal Recipes	❏	❏	❏

CHAPTER 7 REFERENCES AND RESOURCES

Centers for Disease Control and Prevention (CDC). (2011). *Emergency Preparedness and Response*. Retrieved from http://www.bt.cdc.gov/socialmedia/zombies.asp

De'Alesio, R. (2011, September). Centers for Disease Control and Prevention: Preparedness 101: Zombie apocalypse. In *PRNews Platinum PR Awards Issue*. Retrieved from http://www.prnewsonline.com/download/G45318_AI-PBI_PRN_Platinum_Issue_2011.pdf

Escobar, J. F. (2008). *Public relations agency compensation: Enhancing value through best practices*. Retrieved from http://prfirms.org/resources/public-relations-agency-compensation-enhancing-value-through-best-practices

Hallahan, K. (2004). Exhibit 7: Campaigns budget reminder checklist. *Communication campaign/Program organizer*. Retrieved from http:/lamar.colostate.edu/~pr/organizer5.pdf

Hill and Knowlton & Johnson & Johnson. (2011). *text4baby going mobile with pregnancy education*. Retrieved from http://www.prsa.org/SearchResults/view/6BW-1105D05/0/text4baby_Going_Mobile_with_Pregnancy_Education

Pollard, W. (n.d.). Great-Quotes.com. Retrieved from http://www.great-quotes.com/quote/201010

Chapter 8

Writing the Public Relations Plan:
Step 4 Evaluation

One of the great mistakes is to judge policies and programs by their intentions rather than their results.

~ Milton Friedman

This chapter draws on concepts outlined in chapters 5 and 6 to describe the ways in which a public relations program is measured to determine its overall success. It provides readers with a "toolbox" of evaluation methods.

LEARNING OBJECTIVES:

The information presented in this chapter will enable you to:

1. Determine appropriate standards by which to evaluate a public relations plan.

2. Use a variety of evaluation tools to assess the success of a public relations program.

The final questions of any public relations program are always "How did we do?" and "How can we do it better the next time?" The evaluation section of a public relations plan outlines the methods by which those questions are answered. Evaluation allows you to determine the ROI and provides critical information on how the program might be improved in the future.

Although you won't yet know the program results, you must establish the standards of success and the methods to evaluate your achievement of those standards. Remember that decision makers are most interested in the bottom line; they want to know that they will see a meaningful return on investment (ROI). In other words, the plan must yield a tangible gain of some sort to be worth its costs. The evaluation section therefore explains how to determine that gain and offers a projection of your anticipated results. Of course, this means *your evaluation measures must address the extent to which you met your objectives.*

Evaluation is listed as the fourth step of the public relations process, but it is established before you begin, and it's conducted throughout the program. Public relations professionals constantly monitor both the environment and the campaign throughout its implementation. In Chapter 5, we looked at three levels of PR research in Macnamara's Pyramid Model (2011; 2002). As shown again in Figure 8-1, the three levels are Inputs, Outputs, and Outcomes.

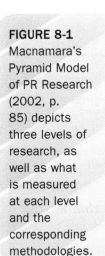

FIGURE 8-1
Macnamara's
Pyramid Model
of PR Research
(2002, p.
85) depicts
three levels of
research, as
well as what
is measured
at each level
and the
corresponding
methodologies.

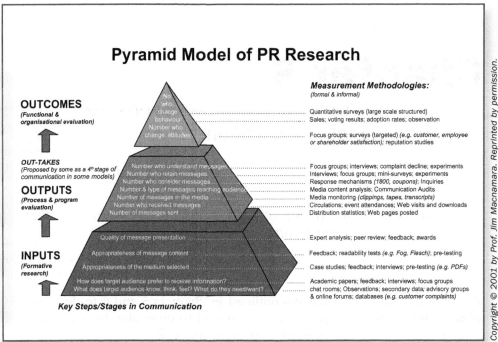

Pyramid Model of PR Research

OUTCOMES
*(Functional &
organisational evaluation)*

No. who change behaviour
Number who change attitudes

OUT-TAKES
*(Proposed by some as a 4th stage of
communication in some models)*

Number who understand messages
Number who retain messages
Number who consider messages
Number & type of messages reaching audience
Number of messages in the media
Number who received messages
Number of messages sent

OUTPUTS
*(Process & program
evaluation)*

Quality of message presentation
Appropriateness of message content
Appropriateness of the medium selected
How does target audience prefer to receive information?
What does target audience know, think, feel? What do they need/want?

INPUTS
*(Formative
research)*

Key Steps/Stages in Communication

Measurement Methodologies:
(formal & informal)

Quantitative surveys (large scale structured)
Sales; voting results; adoption rates; observation

Focus groups; surveys (targeted) *(e.g. customer, employee or shareholder satisfaction)*; reputation studies

Focus groups; interviews; complaint decline; experiments
Interviews; focus groups; mini-surveys; experiments
Response mechanisms *(1800, coupons)*; Inquiries
Media content analysis; Communication Audits
Media monitoring *(clippings, tapes, transcripts)*
Circulations; event attendances; Web visits and downloads
Distribution statistics; Web pages posted

Expert analysis; peer review; feedback; awards

Feedback; readability tests *(e.g. Fog, Flesch)*; pre-testing

Case studies; feedback; interviews; pre-testing *(e.g. PDFs)*

Academic papers; feedback; interviews; focus groups
chat rooms; Observations; secondary data; advisory groups
& online forums; databases *(e.g. customer complaints)*

Note that *formative research* begins at the base of the Pyramid and supports planning and implementation of program *Inputs*. However, the research process is iterative; in other words, it is often repeated or ongoing throughout program implementation and evaluation. By the same token, some *summative research* methods are also used for both Inputs and Outputs. Here, those methods are designed to determine if your program has met your pre-established standards.

Establishing Evaluation Standards

You can develop your evaluation standards in two ways: (1) review your objectives and (2) review your timeline and budget. Clearly, if you complete the program on time and within budget, you are on your way to maximizing the program's ROI. Thus, the Evaluation section of the plan should include these two criteria for success.

If you have written strong objectives, you already have established additional standards. In the Evaluation section, you determine how you will know if you met them. For example, an outcome objective to "improve employee perceptions of transparency by 10 percent by the end of the year" articulates the standard of a 10 percent improvement in employee perceptions with a target date of the end of the year. How will you know if you met that standard? The answer to this single question requires both formative and summative research methods, which focus on the Inputs and Outcomes levels of Macnamara's Pyramid:

1. **Formative Research That Informs Program Inputs.** The methodology would most likely be a preliminary benchmark survey of employees to determine what the baseline attitude is, perhaps as measured with a Likert scale.

2. **Summative Research That Measures Outcomes.** At the end of the year when the program is complete, the results of a second, identical survey can be compared to the first. If the comparison shows a 10 percent increase or more positive perceptions, you have attained or exceeded your objective.

The Research section of your plan describes the methodology for the two surveys. As indicated in Chapter 5, the description should include your sampling method and response rate, the questionnaire construction, and descriptions of the questionnaire items and what they are designed to elicit. This section also should refer the reader to the appendix for a sample of the full questionnaire. If you already described the research methodology in the Research section of your plan, you can simply refer to it in this section.

Most evaluation methods focus on Outputs and Outcomes. However, part of your evaluation should also address your team's activity levels.

Establishing Evaluation Methods

Productivity. One evaluation measure is that of sheer productivity, such as how many letters were written, how many news releases were distributed, how many contacts were made, or how many collateral materials were produced. Chances are good that the client will want to know how the time it paid for was spent, so this is an appropriate measure to include. However, productivity, alone, tells little about the quality of the program. You also need to focus on program Outputs and Outcome.

Program Outputs. As the Pyramid depicts, evaluations of program Outputs include how many people received, understood, retained, or considered your key messages. Examples of these evaluation methods include the following:

- *Press clippings & media tracking.* This is the most widely practiced form of public relations evaluation and measures the extent to which secondary gatekeeping audiences have accepted the messages. Many professional services monitor and report on social media, provide archives of electronic and print media clippings, and monitor broadcast placements. Press clippings are typically reported in terms of "column inches." This means the number of columns across which a given article spans and the length in inches of those columns are multiplied. For example, let's say a press release yielded two stories. One story was 2 columns wide by 5 inches, or 10 column inches. The second story was 3 columns wide by 3 inches, or 9 column inches. The press releases, then, yielded a total of 19 column inches in two print outlets.

- *Media impressions.* These measure the number of individuals who have potentially been exposed to a message. For example, a local newspaper with a circulation of 100,000 readers yields 100,000 media impressions per printed story. Two stories in the same paper yield 200,000 media impressions. Such tools as Internet hits, fan counts, page views, and interaction rates also calculate online or social media impressions.

- *Advertising equivalency.* This calculates the value of message exposure as if it were paid advertising. For example if a one-column by four-inch newspaper ad costs $400, a public relations story of the same size would have an advertising equivalent of $400. This technique can be useful for demonstrating ROI, but it is also controversial, because newspaper stories and advertisements do not necessarily carry the same value. For example, nonpaid newspaper stories carry more credibility than advertisements, but how is the value impacted when a journalist has added negative information to a story?

FIGURE 8-2
Surveys are often the tools used evaluate program Outcomes and Outputs, such as audience comprehension or attitudes.

- *Cost per person.* This calculates the cost of reaching each member of the target public. Here, you refer to your expenses to determine all placement costs and divide that number by the media impressions. The resulting figure can help you discern the cost-effectiveness of your media placements.

- *Attendance.* This involves counting how many individuals attended an event.

- *Response mechanisms.* These include such tools as blog posts, coded coupons, and tracking the number of inquiries or complaints to establish the magnitude of any increase or decrease. These tools measure audience receipt and consideration of the messages.

- *Surveys and interviews.* These determine audience awareness, message retention, and message comprehension.

- *Focus groups and interviews.* These determine message comprehension and acceptance.

Program Outcomes. Ultimately, public relations programs endeavor to influence target publics toward a particular change in behavior, attitude, or opinion, and your objectives will probably include such a measure. Methods for measuring these changes include:

- *Indirect observation.* This includes audience behaviors, such as voting results, sales of products or services, product adoption rates, or donations received.

- *Direct observation.* This covers audience behaviors, such as those in the entertainment industry with sneak movie previews.

- *Surveys and interviews.* These measure consumer satisfaction and opinions.

- *Focus groups.* These are often used to support survey research and delve into consumer opinions.

- *Reputation studies.* As the name implies, these analyze the status of organizational reputation.

As you review each objective, consider as many ways as possible to measure it.

The evaluation tools listed above constitute a partial list of measurement possibilities, and more are on the horizon, as social media continue to evolve. The wise professional stays abreast of new methods and uses those that are most appropriate to demonstrate a program's ROI.

As you review each of your objectives, consider as many ways as possible to measure it. You may use multiple methods to evaluate an objective, and you certainly will use a variety of methods to evaluate the overall program success. As with the rest of your PR plan, clear and concise writing is important, because both you and the client need to know before your campaign is launched how you will evaluate program success.

Writing the Evaluation Section of the Plan

The Evaluation section of the PR plan should be organized according to your goals and objectives. Include at least one measurement for each objective, as well as productivity measures, plus your budgetary and calendar targets. As always, use declarative sentences and strive for economy of words. For example, let's return to our hypothetical outcome objective to "improve employee perceptions of transparency by 10 percent by the end of the year." Your evaluation description for this objective might read something like this:

> Our third objective, which is to improve employee perceptions of transparency by 10 percent by the end of the year, will be measured by pre- and postcampaign employee surveys. The survey design and sampling methods appear in this plan, beginning on page 12 in the section entitled "Research." We anticipate an improvement of at least 10 percent and potentially as much as 15 percent. In addition to the surveys, we will monitor throughout the campaign other indicators of employee perceptions through a series of focus groups and informal interviews.

Note that in this example, three methods of evaluation are planned: (1) pre- and postprogram surveys, (2) focus groups, and (3) informal interviews. The first method measures program Outcomes, and the second and third monitor both Outputs and Outcomes. Note, too, that it is acceptable to write in the first person to avoid excessive use of passive voice.

Tying It All Together

The Evaluation section of a public relations plan outlines the methods you will use to determine the extent to which program objectives are met. Evaluation is important, because when expressed in terms of dollars, it demonstrates ROI to the client, as well as provides information on how the program might be improved in the future. In other words, it becomes part of the research stage for a subsequent program. Evaluation methods can be roughly categorized according to program Inputs, Outputs, and Outcomes. Using multiple methods provides a comprehensive view of a program's success.

Name _____ Date _____

REFLECT AND REVIEW

1. For each of the following, mark the box that correctly identifies an evaluation method as evaluating Input, Output, or Outcomes.

	Input	Output	Outcomes
Mall intercept research	❏	❏	❏
Counting admission tickets	❏	❏	❏
48-hour recall questionnaires	❏	❏	❏
Election exit polls	❏	❏	❏
Content analyses of press clippings	❏	❏	❏
Website hits	❏	❏	❏
Media impressions	❏	❏	❏
Counting coded coupons	❏	❏	❏

2. You have set an objective to increase awareness of the client's brand by 10 percent by the end of the campaign. What is your standard for evaluation?

_____

3. How many evaluation methods can you identify that will help you determine your success? Be specific.

_____

_____

_____

_____

4. You plan to send two news releases to a newspaper with a circulation of 500,000. If both items are printed, how many media impressions have you made? Show your calculation below.

_____

_____

_____

_____

CHAPTER 8 REFERENCES AND RESOURCES

Friedman, M. (1975, December 7). *Richard Heffner's Open Mind* [television interview program]. New York: WNET.

Macnamara, J. R. (2011, December 9). PR metrics. *Whitepaper for the International Association for the Measurement and Evaluation of Communication.* Retrieved from http://amecorg.com/wp-content/uploads/2011/10/PR-Metrics-Paper.pdf

Macnamara, J. (2002). Research and evaluation. In C. Tymson & P. Lazar, *The New Australian and New Zealand Public Relations Manual* (pp. 100–134). Sydney: Tymson Communications.

Chapter 9
Reporting the Public Relations Program Results

Clear? Huh! Why a four-year-old child could understand this report. Run out and find me a four-year-old child. I can't make head or tail out of it.

~Groucho Marx as Rufus T. Firefly in Duck Soup

This chapter outlines the final report of a public relations program, including organization of materials, analysis, and conclusions. Readers will learn how to incorporate information from a public relations plan into a report of completed work, as well as write results and conclusions.

LEARNING OBJECTIVES

The information presented in this chapter will enable you to:

1. Modify the language of a public relations plan for incorporation into a final program report.

2. Structure and organize a readable and coherent final program report.

Writing the Final Report

The final report for your public relations program describes the campaign from start to finish. It should outline the client's background, the problem you identified, your original goals and objectives, the steps you took to meet those goals and objectives, your target publics, key messages, strategies, tools and tactics, your timeline, budget, and all the tools you used to execute and evaluate your campaign. As with your original proposal, you should use numbered pages, index tabs, and subheads throughout to guide the reader through the materials. Remember: For any writing project, including this one, the burden is on you to make sure the reader can follow your key points. The good news is that a good chunk of your final report is already written.

Recycling the PR Plan

Your original public relations plan includes much of the information you need, so you already have a significant portion of the final report written. However, bear in mind that *you are now reporting something you did (past tense), not something you propose to do (future tense).* You therefore *must* change all applicable verb tenses in the PR plan from future tense to past tense. Failure to do so indicates a lack of interest and professionalism.

FIGURE 9-1.
Most of a public relations plan can be recycled to form the bulk of a final report.

The next two sections offer "before" and "after" examples of what could be the Implementation section in a public relations plan and how the language can be modified for a final report. The example is adapted from a 2010 interview with Chip McComb, New Media Specialist at Kiwanis International Foundation, by a representative of the About.Com *Nonprofit Guide* (2010). Note that in the second, "past tense" example, missed target dates are reported, along the revised target dates.

Language for a Public Relations Plan (Future Tense Activities)

Our first objective, which is to reward a nonprofit organization with a significant grant, will be implemented in the spring. During the period of March 1 through April 1, we will ask Facebook users to nominate their favorite charities and indicate (through a popular vote) which of the nominated charities deserve to win. To nominate a charity, a user must have a Facebook account and they must grant us access to their Facebook profile. During this initial period, we anticipate that approximately 500,000 charities will be nominated. On April 2, the 100 charities that receive the most votes will be awarded a grant and then given the opportunity to compete for the top two grant awards. Submissions will be due on May 1, the charities' big ideas will be announced on May 10, and the second round of voting by the Facebook community will begin on May 15. The second voting period will end 10 days later on May 25, and the grants will be awarded to the winning charities by June 1.

The guidelines are simple. The nonprofit nominee must be a 501(c)3 organization with a modest operating budget of less than $1 million. To win the top grant the nominee must tell the Facebook community how it would use the grant using 3,000 words or less, a few photos, and a single video not to exceed five minutes.

Language for a Final Report (Past Tense Activities)

Our first objective, which was to reward a nonprofit organization with a significant grant, was implemented in the spring. During the period of March 1 through April 1, we asked Facebook users to nominate their favorite charities and indicate (through a popular vote) which of the nominated charities deserved to win. To nominate a charity, a user must have had a Facebook account and they must have granted us access to their Facebook profile. During this initial period, we anticipated that approximately 500,000 charities would be nominated. On April 2, the 100 charities that received the most votes were awarded a grant and given the opportunity to compete for the top two grant awards. Submissions were due on May 1. The charities' big ideas were announced on May 15, a five-day delay from the original May 10 target, and the second round of voting by the Facebook community began on May 20, again five days later than originally planned. The second voting period ended 10 days later on May 30, and the grants were awarded to the winning charities.

The guidelines were simple. The nonprofit nominee had to be a 501(c)3 organization with a modest operating budget of less than $1 million. To win the top grant, the nominee told the Facebook community how it would use the grant using 3,000 words or less, a few photos, and a single video not to exceed five minutes.

Once you've reworded your plan with appropriate language, you need to do minimal restructuring to adapt it to the final report. The following outline will help you organize the document.

Structuring the Final Report

As is the case with a public relations proposal, a letter of transmittal and a one- or two-page executive summary accompany the final report. The report body is structured much the same as a PR plan. The structure is based on the four steps of the public relations process, as shown in the following outline. Note that the bulk of the report is drawn from the original plan. Only the section for conclusions, part of the appendix, and a segment of the evaluation section, which now includes program results, are new. The new elements appear as ***bold italics*** in the outline below.

I. Introduction

    A. Brief background of the client organization

    B. Description of who conducted the program and why

    C. Overview of the original problems and potential solutions

    D. Rationale for public relations as a cost-effective approach to the problem

II. Problem Statement

    A. Research

        1. Situation analysis

            a. Political, Economic, Social, and Technological issues faced by the client (PEST Analysis)

            b. Client Strengths, Weaknesses, Opportunities, and Threats (SWOT Analysis)

            c. Problem Statement

2. Analysis of key publics

   a. Demographics

   b. Psychographics

   c. Influencers and self interests

   d. Relationships to the client

III. Work Statement

A. Planning

   1. Goals & objectives

   2. Key messages for each key public

     a. Primary publics

     b. Secondary publics

B. Implementation

   1. Strategies to reach each key public

   2. Tools & tactics to be used

   3. Calendar

   4. Budget

C. Evaluation

   1. Evaluation criteria

   2. Evaluation tools and measurements

   3. Program results

IV. Conclusions

   A. Summary of problems and successes

   B. Suggestions for future improvement

   C. Lessons learned

V. Appendix

   A. Samples of all completed deliverables (e.g., brochures, newsletters, websites, news releases)

   B. Media lists and other working documents

   C. *NOTE: Students should include an alphabetized, detailed list of references that you used for your research (APA or MLA style)*

The following three sections describe the contents of the elements that are newly written for the final report.

FIGURE 9-2.
The final report demonstrates to the client how well your objectives were met and if the PR program yielded an adequate Return on Investment.

Evaluation

As it did in the original plan, the Evaluation section describes the tools that were used to assess program success for each objective. Now, however, you are reporting not only the methods, but also the results. Be careful in this section to avoid drawing conclusions or interpreting the findings. You are only reporting the findings of your summative research. For example, you report the completion date and the final costs, as well as their significance, in terms of your projected timeline and budget. Similarly, if a postcampaign survey indicates an 8 percent increase in awareness of the client's mission, this section reports the increase, in terms of the original objective. However, implications for future campaigns and explanations of unexpected results appear only in the subsequent Conclusions section.

Conclusions

The Conclusions section of the final report comprises three subsections. First, it opens with an introductory paragraph that summarizes the campaign and reports any challenges that your team encountered throughout the implementation of the program, as well as how those challenges were overcome.

Second, the Conclusions section addresses the extent to which the planned goals and objectives were met, based on the results you reported in the Evaluation section. This subsection is the heart of your report, and it is what the client most wants to know. It must answer three fundamental questions:

1. To what extent were the stated goals and objectives met?

2. Did you meet your projected target dates and stay within budget?

3. What is the return on investment?

Finally, the Conclusions section offers suggestions on how the program might be improved, should it be done again in the future. When reporting the lessons learned, take care to stay focused on the program, and not on the client's behaviors. Similar to reporting the client's weaknesses in the SWOT analysis, do not insult the client here. You are analyzing only the program, and you want to end the endeavor on good terms with your client, even if this client happens to be a difficult one.

The final program report must answer three fundamental questions: (1) To what extent were the stated goals and objectives met? (2) Did you meet your projected target dates and stay within budget? (3) What is the return on investment?

Appendix

The Appendix of the report is virtually identical to that of the proposal, but now it includes samples of materials that were ultimately produced and used in the campaign, rather than mockups of proposed pieces. This section should contain only representative samples, not every item you prepared. For example, if you sent press releases to 20 media outlets, you should list the outlets in your media list and provide a single, illustrative news release.

Tying It All Together

The final report of a public relations program is based on the PR plan. Much of the PR plan can be revised to report the completed program. The final report describes (1) the client's original situation, (2) the problem *or* opportunity that the program addressed, (3) the organizational and public relations goals and objectives, (4) the target audiences, (5) the key messages, (6) the strategies, tactics, and tools that were chosen to reach the target audiences, (7) how the tools and tactics were implemented, (8) how the outcomes were measured, and most importantly, (9) the ROI.

Public relations is a strategic endeavor, and your final report should reflect that. Strategic public relations requires thoughtful, research-based and ethical decision making, as well as creativity, a deep understanding of target audiences, and effective ways in which to reach those audiences. Delivering a solid public relations campaign calls for careful planning and management of time, resources, and personnel. Finally, attention to detail and careful follow-through are essential for excellent public relations programs.

Name _____ Date _____

REFLECT AND REVIEW

1. In which section of a final program report should a sample brochure be placed?

   _____

2. In which section of a final program report is the ROI reported?

   _____

3. What three basic questions should the final program report answer?

   a. _____

   b. _____

   c. _____

CHAPTER 9 REFERENCES AND RESOURCES

Fritz, J. (2010, February 22). *Using social media to win charity competitions: How email trumped social media for Kiwanis in the Chase Giving Contest.* Retrieved from http://nonprofit.about.com/od/fundraising/a/kiwanisandchase.htm

Kalmar, B., Ruby, H., Sheekman, A., & Perrin, N. (1933). *Duck Soup.* Quoted by the Internet Movie Database website. Retrieved from http://www.imdb.com/title/tt0023969

Chapter 10
Preparing and Delivering Professional Presentations

A lot of times, people don't know what they want until you show it to them.

~Steve Jobs

This chapter addresses preparation, structure, and timing of formal business presentations. Topics include appropriate dress, and development and use of effective visual aids.

LEARNING OBJECTIVES

The information presented in this chapter will enable you to:

1. Deliver a formal oral presentation of a public relations proposal or final report.

2. Develop effective visual aids for a formal presentation.

3. Select appropriate, professional attire for a formal presentation.

Public relations professionals routinely deliver formal and informal oral presentations. Once you have written a public relations plan or proposal, for example, you may need to present it to decision makers, either alone or as part of a team. The success of your in-person performance can mean the difference between getting approval to proceed and never seeing the plan implemented. It's therefore critical that you carefully consider how you can convincingly present your work. Giving a presentation can be a daunting prospect, but with proper preparation, you can look forward to a fruitful experience.

Preparing for your presentation involves three fundamental things: (1) organization and manner of presenting the material, (2) effective visual aids, and (3) appropriate attire. The following sections address each topic in turn.

Organizing the Presentation Material

The most frequently used structure of a presentation follows a three-part organization: (1) introduction, (2) body, and (3) conclusion. In general, the content of these three components should follow the old saying, "Tell 'em what you're going to tell 'em; tell 'em; then tell 'em what you told 'em." This redundancy helps your audience absorb and retain the information.

Tell ' Em What You're Going To Tell ' Em

The introduction should be about 10 percent of your allotted time. It is designed to do two things: (1) get the audience's attention and (2) orient the audience to your topic. Open the presentation with some compelling attention-getting device, such as a rhetorical question, a startling statistic, or an interesting related story. Then, as quickly as possible, state the goal or purpose of the presentation and provide an overview of the key ideas you plan to present. If it is a group presentation, introduce your team members. If the presentation is an invited one resulting from a written proposal, a brief thank-you to the client is also appropriate.

Tell ' Em

The body of your presentation should use about 80 percent of the allotted time. Think carefully about the major themes you want to present. Your time is probably limited, so choose wisely and, as with any communication, consider what your target audience most wants to know. Bear in mind that although you should follow the general structure of the document you are presenting, you do not have time to cover every detail. If you're presenting a proposal, focus on the strategy, costs, time frame, and potential return on investment (ROI). For a final report, highlight how well the objectives were met and the ROI.

Tell ' Em What You Told ' Em

The last 10 percent or so of your presentation time should summarize your key points and "close the loop" by referring back to your introductory attention-getter. If you are presenting a proposal of public relations work, your presentation should close with an invitation to the client to accept the proposal and begin the program.

Whether the presentation is a proposal or a final program report, thank the client for allowing you the time to present your work. Finally, open the presentation to questions, comments, or discussion. It is critical that you end on a positive note, and that you leave the client with a positive impression of your team and your work.

FIGURE 10-1. It pays to show enthusiasm and maintain eye contact with the audience when giving a public relations presentation.

How To Tell ' Em

The tone of your presentation is almost as important as the content. You will never convince the client that your proposal is sound or that your work is effective if you don't believe it and demonstrate that belief. Show enthusiasm, use appropriate language and intonation, and maintain eye contact with audience members. Help your audience visualize the outcomes you are proposing or reporting. Here are a few dos and don'ts to keep in mind:

Do:

- Think ahead and visualize your presentation. Mental rehearsal helps you make the presentation as smooth as possible.

- Practice. Practice with your teammates, practice in front of a mirror, practice using your visual aids, and practice answering questions that might be asked.

- Be conscious of your rate of speech. It's easy to talk too fast or mumble when you are nervous.

- Know your material inside and out. If you are presenting as part of a team, know everyone's role, so you can step in should a teammate be unable to attend at the last minute.

- Make eye contact with all audience members and look attentive when other teammates are presenting.

- Present sufficient detail, but avoid overwhelming the audience with minutiae.

- Prepare the room in advance, if possible. Test the equipment. Adjust the lighting and seating arrangement for maximum effectiveness.

- Prepare alternative modes of presenting. Have functioning backup plans for everything.

- Incorporate creativity.

- Provide a hard copy of a proposal or program report to the client and refer to the appropriate page numbers as you move through the content. It's often effective to provide page cues on your visual aids to help the client navigate the document with you.

Don't:

- Provide handouts or leave-behinds until after the presentation is complete. You want to keep the client focused on you and your presentation. However, handing out the proposal or final report is an exception to this rule, because your presentation is intended to walk the client through the key elements of the document.

- Fidget, slouch, or look uninterested if a teammate is presenting.

- Use inappropriate language for the audience. For example, there is no place for the phrase "you guys" in a formal business presentation.

- Vocalize your pauses or verbal missteps with meaningless expressions, such as "um," "uh," or "like." These verbal insertions are known as *speech disfluencies*, and they suggest to the audience that you are poorly prepared, immature, uncertain, or all three.

- Face the screen when using projected visual aids. The screen doesn't care what you have to say. Keep your eyes on the audience.

- Read or memorize the material unless you have great acting ability. Reading and memorization tend to result in a monotone delivery, which will destroy your credibility as a knowledgeable and enthusiastic public relations professional.

- Worry about being nervous. Use your nerves to your advantage. That nervous edge can add energy to your presentation. Remember, the audience is rooting for you to do well.

- Lose track of time. As a matter of professionalism and courtesy, be punctual, both at the start and at the end of your presentation.

- Block your visual aids. Take care to place yourself in such a way that everyone in the room can see them.

- Oversell. You are using the *central route* to persuasion, which is based on the strength of your evidence. Make your case, encourage acceptance, and *stop*.

Once you have outlined your presentation and determined how you will deliver it, you need to develop ways to add interest or clarify complex ideas. One way to do both of those things is with the use of visual aids.

Preparing Effective Visual Aids

The first thing to consider when planning visual aids is what they're designed to do. They should *enhance* and *illuminate* your presentation; they should not repeat it, nor should they be expected to tell the story for you. Think carefully about the presentation's purpose and key concepts and make every visual aid meaningful. Be judicious with your use of technology, because it can depersonalize the overall impact of your exposition. If you're using presentation software such as Apple Keynote or Microsoft PowerPoint or an online presentation editor such as the Prezi website, avoid overwhelming the viewer with elaborate transitions or animations or sounds. Remember, just because you *can* do something doesn't mean you *should*.

Make sure that every slide, every photo, every graph, every table, and every video adds meaning to what you plan to say. Use appropriate graphics to clarify and illuminate your content and have descriptive, easy-to-read labels. For example, trends over time are best illustrated with line graphs, while pie charts are better suited for showing demographic or financial distributions.

A rule of thumb for developing effective visual aids is widely known as the "Three Bs." Make them **Big**, **Bold**, and **Brief**.

Big visual aids include (1) large, readable fonts, generally, around 20 points for relatively intimate venues and 48 points or more for large venues and (2) appropriately scaled displays and models. For example, a demonstration of threading a needle would be completely ineffective with a standard sewing needle and thread. The audience would not be able to discern adequate detail to understand the process. For this demonstration to be effective, you would need to use an oversized model of a needle and length of string or even rope as the thread. Similarly, projected images, videos, etc., should be large enough to see well from a distance.

Bold visuals enhance the readability of labels and textual information. Use boldface, sans serif fonts, which are easier to read when projected on a screen. Consider using the built-in tools of PowerPoint, Keynote, or the Prezi presentation website for

FIGURES 10-2. Demographic changes over time are best shown as a line graph, as shown in Figure 10-2a. A snapshot of demographic distribution at one point in time is better illustrated as a pie chart like the one shown in Figure 10-2b.

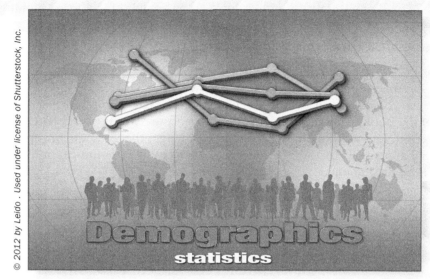

FIGURE 10-2a

FIGURE 10-2b

selective disclosure, rather than displaying an entire slide at once. Timed properly, this helps your audience focus on what you are saying. Color choices also affect readability. Every step away from black-and-white is a step away from readability. Be sure to use high-contrast text, one or two fonts at the most, and pleasing color schemes. Some nice turnkey templates are available on the Web and within Microsoft PowerPoint or Apple Keynote.

Brief visual aids are visually and textually straightforward. Be sure each slide has plenty of white space, including generous margins and line spacing. Use bullet points on projected slides and limit them to three or four per slide. A telegraphic style of 5–7-word phrases, omitting modifiers and articles ("a," "an," "the"), is more effective than complete sentences, and parallel construction adds cohesion and clarity to the text.

Cluttered backgrounds, busy designs, and multiple nonessential images are likely to distract the viewer. In other words, the key to successful visual aids is keeping everything as fresh and uncomplicated as possible. Be sure to proofread everything to avoid the embarrassment of a misspelling typo glaring on the screen to your client. Of course, equally important to a great looking presentation is a great looking presenter.

Dressing for a Formal Business Presentation

In 1975, John T. Malloy published a research-based, best-selling book entitled *Dress for Success*, which proposed that how a person dressed affected in a real way the ability to succeed in business. Thirteen years later, he published an updated version of the book. Although the cuts of suits and the width of ties had changed during that period, and although they continue to change, the general concept has not. Your personal appearance matters. Think of it as a form of communication that must appeal to your target audience.

Fashion fades; only style remains the same.

~Coco Chanel

As you contemplate your business wardrobe, it's important to keep in mind that dressing for success in business has nothing to do with fashion or current trends. It is about adopting the uniform of corporate America. Whether it is to your personal taste or not, if you want to be taken seriously in a professional environment, you need to dress as a serious professional. This section describes how to do that.

If you are engaging in a formal business presentation, such as that for a public relations proposal, you need to dress accordingly. That means you must dress in *formal business attire*, not "business casual" clothing. The look is one of authority and power.

The Fundamentals

Conservative, well-tailored suits in natural fibers such as wool or silk constitute the basis of the formal business wardrobe. Buy the best you can afford. This is an investment in your future, and a conservative, timeless cut will last for years. Navy, black, charcoal, and subtle pinstripes are typically viewed as being the most formal colors and patterns. They also have the advantage of being neutral enough to work with a broad variety of shirts or blouses and accessories. Shirts or blouses should be white or pastel with collars and long sleeves.

Considerations for Women

Women's skirts must be at least knee-length, and the jacket should be well-fitted, hip or fingertip length, and button all the way down. Tuck in the blouse. It should not be visible below the jacket's bottom edge. Take care that your clothing fits well, with no stretched fabric or pulls between buttons and no discernible cleavage. Select conservative, minimal jewelry, close-toed shoes with medium heels, and skin-toned or black stockings. Be sure your hair is neatly styled and use a neutral color palette for makeup and nails. A small portfolio completes a refined, professional look.

FIGURE 10-3   FIGURE 10-4

What you **say**
is only **half** the interview.

No excess jewelry
Neatly styled hair
No excess makeup
No excessive perfume
Dress shirt
Jacket
Long skirt
Neat, trimmed nails
Small portfolio
Skin-toned nylons
Close-toed shoes
No spiked heels

Dress Accordingly.

Cal State Fullerton Career Center   LH-208 • www.fullerton.edu/career • (657) 278-3121

Courtesy of Callifornia State University Fullerton Career Center. Illustration by Ray Fero.

What you **say**
is only **half** the interview.

Clean-cut hairstyle
Clean shaven face
No excessive cologne
Deodorant
Dark colored suit
Collared dress shirt
Subdued tie
No excess jewelry
Small portfolio
Dress slacks
Black dress shoes & socks

Dress Accordingly.

Cal State Fullerton Career Center   LH-208 • www.fullerton.edu/career • (657) 278-3121

Courtesy of California State University Fullerton Career Center. Illustration by Ray Fero.

Considerations for Men

Men should have a clean-cut, conservative hairstyle. Although a clean-shaven look is favored, minimal, neatly trimmed facial hair is acceptable. Your tie can have a subtle pattern or stripe, but should be fairly subdued. A deep, rich red, which is often seen as a "power" color, is fine. Long-sleeved shirts are more formal than short-sleeved shirts, and should be pressed and crisp looking. You should wear well-polished, black dress shoes and dark socks to match your suit.

The Devil Is in the Details

Details can make or break a presentation, and they can do the same for your professional look. Keep all jewelry conservative and wear very little. Do not wear religious or political emblems. Avoid wearing any fragrances, in case a decision maker suffers from allergies, but use plenty of deodorant. Make sure nails are neatly trimmed and that everything is clean and well pressed.

A sophisticated, professional look keeps the focus on the substance of your message.

If all of this sounds boring, that's not a bad thing. Save your more interesting wardrobe choices for date night. Remember that in a professional setting, you want the audience to pay attention to what you have to say, not how you look. Even a minor wardrobe misstep can distract your audience and undermine your credibility, but a sophisticated, professional look keeps the focus on the substance of your message.

Tying It All Together

Public relations professionals often do a lot of public speaking, both in relaxed settings and in formal settings. All oral presentations should be well prepared, organized, and rehearsed. Visual aids should be big, bold, and brief to clarify and complement the content of any presentation. Formal presentations require formal business attire to convey an image of authority and credibility.

REFLECT AND REVIEW

1. What percent of the time allotted for an oral presentation should be devoted to the introduction and the conclusion combined?

   _____

2. What two things should a presentation's introduction accomplish?

   a. _____

   b. _____

3. What content should you include in the introduction to a presentation?

   _____

   _____

   _____

4. Why should you "Tell 'em what you're going to tell 'em; tell 'em; and tell 'em what you told 'em?"

   _____

   _____

5. What are three characteristics of effective visual aids? Be specific and explain each.

   a. _____

   b. _____

   c. _____

CHAPTER 10 REFERENCES AND RESOURCES

AccuConference. (n.d.). *Undeniable conference impact: Using visual aids.* Henderson, NV: Author. Retrieved from http://www.accuconference.com/resources/conference-impact.aspx

Malloy, J. T. (1988). *John T. Malloy's new dress for success.* New York: Warner Books.

Reinhardt, A. (1998, May). Steve Jobs: 'There's sanity returning.' *BusinessWeek.* Retrieved from http://www.businessweek.com/1998/21/b3579165.htm

Rice On-line Writing Lab. (n.d.). *Designing effective oral presentations.* Henderson, NV: AccuConference. Retrieved from http://www.accuconference.com/resources/conference-impact.aspx

Toastmasters International. (n.d.). *Need help giving a speech?* Mission Viejo, CA: Author. Retrieved from http://www.toastmasters.org/MainMenuCategories/FreeResources/NeedHelpGivingaSpeech.aspx

APPENDIX 1: PUBLIC RELATIONS SOCIETY CODE OF ETHICS

Preamble

Public Relations Society of America Member Code of Ethics 2000

- Professional Values
- Principles of Conduct
- Commitment and Compliance

This Code applies to PRSA members. The Code is designed to be a useful guide for PRSA members as they carry out their ethical responsibilities. This document is designed to anticipate and accommodate, by precedent, ethical challenges that may arise. The scenarios outlined in the Code provision are actual examples of misconduct. More will be added as experience with the Code occurs.

The Public Relations Society of America (PRSA) is committed to ethical practices. The level of public trust PRSA members seek, as we serve the public good, means we have taken on a special obligation to operate ethically.

The value of member reputation depends upon the ethical conduct of everyone affiliated with the Public Relations Society of America. Each of us sets an example for each other—as well as other professionals—by our pursuit of excellence with powerful standards of performance, professionalism, and ethical conduct.

Emphasis on enforcement of the Code has been eliminated. But, the PRSA Board of Directors retains the right to bar from membership or expel from the Society any individual who has been or is sanctioned by a government agency or convicted in a court of law of an action that is in violation of this Code.

Ethical practice is the most important obligation of a PRSA member. We view the Member Code of Ethics as a model for other professions, organizations, and professionals.

PRSA Member Statement of Professional Values

This statement presents the core values of PRSA members and, more broadly, of the public relations profession. These values provide the foundation for the Member Code of Ethics and set the industry standard for the professional practice of public relations. These values are the fundamental beliefs that guide our behaviors and decision-making process. We believe our professional values are vital to the integrity of the profession as a whole.

Advocacy

We serve the public interest by acting as responsible advocates for those we represent. We provide a voice in the marketplace of ideas, facts, and viewpoints to aid informed public debate.

Honesty

We adhere to the highest standards of accuracy and truth in advancing the interests of those we represent and in communicating with the public.

Expertise

We acquire and responsibly use specialized knowledge and experience. We advance the profession through continued professional development, research, and education. We build mutual understanding, credibility, and relationships among a wide array of institutions and audiences.

Independence

We provide objective counsel to those we represent. We are accountable for our actions.

Loyalty

We are faithful to those we represent, while honoring our obligation to serve the public interest.

Fairness

We deal fairly with clients, employers, competitors, peers, vendors, the media, and the general public. We respect all opinions and support the right of free expression.

PRSA Code Provisions

Free Flow of Information

Core Principle: Protecting and advancing the free flow of accurate and truthful information is essential to serving the public interest and contributing to informed decision making in a democratic society.

Intent

To maintain the integrity of relationships with the media, government officials, and the public.

To aid informed decision making.

Guidelines

A member shall:

Preserve the integrity of the process of communication.

Be honest and accurate in all communications.

Act promptly to correct erroneous communications for which the practitioner is responsible.

Preserve the free flow of unprejudiced information when giving or receiving gifts by ensuring that gifts are nominal, legal, and infrequent.

Examples of Improper Conduct Under This Provision

A member representing a ski manufacturer gives a pair of expensive racing skis to a sports magazine columnist to influence the columnist to write favorable articles about the product.

A member entertains a government official beyond legal limits and/or in violation of government reporting requirements.

Competition

Core Principle: Promoting healthy and fair competition among professionals preserves an ethical climate while fostering a robust business environment.

Intent

To promote respect and fair competition among public relations professionals.

To serve the public interest by providing the widest choice of practitioner options.

Guidelines

A member shall:

Follow ethical hiring practices designed to respect free and open competition without deliberately undermining a competitor.

Preserve intellectual property rights in the marketplace.

Examples of Improper Conduct Under This Provision

A member employed by a "client organization" shares helpful information with a counseling firm that is competing with others for the organization's business.

A member spreads malicious and unfounded rumors about a competitor in order to alienate the competitor's clients and employees in a ploy to recruit people and business.

Disclosure Of Information

Core Principle: Open communication fosters informed decision making in a democratic society.

Intent

To build trust with the public by revealing all information needed for responsible decision making.

Guidelines

A member shall:

Be honest and accurate in all communications.

Act promptly to correct erroneous communications for which the member is responsible.

Investigate the truthfulness and accuracy of information released on behalf of those represented.

Reveal the sponsors for causes and interests represented.

Disclose financial interest (such as stock ownership) in a client's organization.

Avoid deceptive practices.

Examples of Improper Conduct Under This Provision

Front groups: A member implements "grassroots" campaigns or letter-writing campaigns to legislators on behalf of undisclosed interest groups.

Lying by omission: A practitioner for a corporation knowingly fails to release financial information, giving a misleading impression of the corporation's performance.

A member discovers inaccurate information disseminated via a website or media kit and does not correct the information.

A member deceives the public by employing people to pose as volunteers to speak at public hearings and participate in "grassroots" campaigns.

Safeguarding Confidences

Core Principle: Client trust requires appropriate protection of confidential and private information.

Intent

To protect the privacy rights of clients, organizations, and individuals by safeguarding confidential information.

Guidelines
A member shall:

Safeguard the confidences and privacy rights of present, former, and prospective clients and employees.

Protect privileged, confidential, or insider information gained from a client or organization.

Immediately advise an appropriate authority if a member discovers that confidential information is being divulged by an employee of a client company or organization.

Examples of Improper Conduct Under This Provision
A member changes jobs, takes confidential information, and uses that information in the new position to the detriment of the former employer.

A member intentionally leaks proprietary information to the detriment of some other party.

Conflicts of Interest

Core Principle: Avoiding real, potential, or perceived conflicts of interest builds the trust of clients, employers, and the publics.

Intent
To earn trust and mutual respect with clients or employers.

To build trust with the public by avoiding or ending situations that put one's personal or professional interests in conflict with society's interests.

Guidelines
A member shall:

Act in the best interests of the client or employer, even subordinating the member's personal interests.

Avoid actions and circumstances that may appear to compromise good business judgment or create a conflict between personal and professional interests.

Disclose promptly any existing or potential conflict of interest to affected clients or organizations.

Encourage clients and customers to determine if a conflict exists after notifying all affected parties.

Examples of Improper Conduct Under This Provision
The member fails to disclose that he or she has a strong financial interest in a client's chief competitor.

The member represents a "competitor company" or a "conflicting interest" without informing a prospective client.

Enhancing the Profession

Core Principle: Public relations professionals work constantly to strengthen the public's trust in the profession.

Intent
To build respect and credibility with the public for the profession of public relations.

To improve, adapt, and expand professional practices.

Guidelines

A member shall:

Acknowledge that there is an obligation to protect and enhance the profession.

Keep informed and educated about practices in the profession to ensure ethical conduct.

Actively pursue personal professional development.

Decline representation of clients or organizations that urge or require actions contrary to this Code.

Accurately define what public relations activities can accomplish.

Counsel subordinates in proper ethical decision making.

Require that subordinates adhere to the ethical requirements of the Code.

Report ethical violations, whether committed by PRSA members or not, to the appropriate authority.

Examples of Improper Conduct Under This Provision

A PRSA member declares publicly that a product the client sells is safe, without disclosing evidence to the contrary.

A member initially assigns some questionable client work to a nonmember practitioner to avoid the ethical obligation of PRSA membership.

PRSA Member Code of Ethics Pledge

I pledge:

To conduct myself professionally, with truth, accuracy, fairness, and responsibility to the public; To improve my individual competence and advance the knowledge and proficiency of the profession through continuing research and education; And to adhere to the articles of the Member Code of Ethics 2000 for the practice of public relations as adopted by the governing Assembly of the Public Relations Society of America.

I understand and accept that there is a consequence for misconduct, up to and including membership revocation.

And, I understand that those who have been or are sanctioned by a government agency or convicted in a court of law of an action that is in violation of this Code may be barred from membership or expelled from the Society.

_____

Signature

_____

Date

APPENDIX 2: IABC CODE OF ETHICS FOR PROFESSIONAL COMMUNICATORS

Preface

Because hundreds of thousands of business communicators worldwide engage in activities that affect the lives of millions of people, and because this power carries with it significant social responsibilities, the International Association of Business Communicators developed the Code of Ethics for Professional Communicators.

The Code is based on three different yet interrelated principles of professional communication that apply throughout the world.

These principles assume that just societies are governed by a profound respect for human rights and the rule of law; that ethics, the criteria for determining what is right and wrong, can be agreed upon by members of an organization; and, that understanding matters of taste requires sensitivity to cultural norms.

These principles are essential:

- Professional communication is legal.

- Professional communication is ethical.

- Professional communication is in good taste.

Recognizing these principles, members of IABC will:

- Engage in communication that is not only legal but also ethical and sensitive to cultural values and beliefs;

- Engage in truthful, accurate and fair communication that facilitates respect and mutual understanding;

- adhere to the following articles of the IABC Code of Ethics for Professional Communicators.

Because conditions in the world are constantly changing, members of IABC will work to improve their individual competence and to increase the body of knowledge in the field with research and education.

Articles

1. Professional communicators uphold the credibility and dignity of their profession by practicing honest, candid and timely communication and by fostering the free flow of essential information in accord with the public interest.

2. Professional communicators disseminate accurate information and promptly correct any erroneous communication for which they may be responsible.

3. Professional communicators understand and support the principles of free speech, freedom of assembly, and access to an open marketplace of ideas and act accordingly.

4. Professional communicators are sensitive to cultural values and beliefs and engage in fair and balanced communication activities that foster and encourage mutual understanding.

5. Professional communicators refrain from taking part in any undertaking which the communicator considers to be unethical.

6. Professional communicators obey laws and public policies governing their professional activities and are sensitive to the spirit of all laws and regulations and, should any law or public policy be violated, for whatever reason, act promptly to correct the situation.

7. Professional communicators give credit for unique expressions borrowed from others and identify the sources and purposes of all information disseminated to the public.

8. Professional communicators protect confidential information and, at the same time, comply with all legal requirements for the disclosure of information affecting the welfare of others.

9. Professional communicators do not use confidential information gained as a result of professional activities for personal benefit and do not represent conflicting or competing interests without written consent of those involved.

10. Professional communicators do not accept undisclosed gifts or payments for professional services from anyone other than a client or employer.

11. Professional communicators do not guarantee results that are beyond the power of the practitioner to deliver.

12. Professional communicators are honest not only with others but also, and most importantly, with themselves as individuals; for a professional communicator seeks the truth and speaks that truth first to the self.

Enforcement and Communication of The IABC Code of Ethics

IABC fosters compliance with its Code by engaging in global communication campaigns rather than through negative sanctions. However, in keeping with the sixth article of the IABC Code, members of IABC who are found guilty by an appropriate governmental agency or judicial body of violating laws and public policies governing their professional activities may have their membership terminated by the IABC executive board following procedures set forth in the association's bylaws.

IABC encourages the widest possible communication about its Code.

The IABC Code of Ethics for Professional Communicators is published in several languages and is freely available to all: Permission is hereby granted to any individual or organization wishing to copy and incorporate all or part of the IABC Code into personal and corporate codes, with the understanding that appropriate credit be given to IABC in any publication of such codes.

The IABC Code is published on the association's website. The association's bimonthly magazine, *Communication World*, publishes periodic articles dealing with ethical issues. At least one session at the association's annual conference is devoted to ethics. The international headquarters of IABC, through its professional development activities, encourages and supports efforts by IABC student chapters, professional chapters, and regions to conduct meetings and workshops devoted to the topic of ethics and the IABC Code. New and renewing members of IABC sign the following statement as part of their application: "I have reviewed and understand the IABC Code of Ethics for Professional Communicators."

As a service to communicators worldwide, inquiries about ethics and questions or comments about the IABC Code may be addressed to members of the IABC Ethics Committee. The IABC Ethics Committee is composed of at least three accredited members of IABC who serve staggered three-year terms. Other IABC members may serve on the committee with the approval of the IABC executive committee. The functions of the Ethics Committee are to assist with professional development activities dealing with ethics and to offer advice and assistance to individual communicators regarding specific ethical situations.

While discretion will be used in handling all inquiries about ethics, absolute confidentiality cannot be guaranteed. Those wishing more information about the IABC Code or specific advice about ethics are encouraged to contact IABC World Headquarters (601 Montgomery Street, Suite 1900, San Francisco, CA 94111 USA; phone, +1 415.544.4700; fax, +1 415.544.4747).

APPENDIX 3: AMERICAN MARKETING ASSOCIATION STATEMENT OF ETHICS

Ethical Norms and Values for Marketers

Preamble

The American Marketing Association commits itself to promoting the highest standard of professional ethical norms and values for its members (practitioners, academics and students). Norms are established standards of conduct that are expected and maintained by society and/or professional organizations. Values represent the collective conception of what communities find desirable, important and morally proper. Values also serve as the criteria for evaluating our own personal actions and the actions of others. As marketers, we recognize that we not only serve our organizations but also act as stewards of society in creating, facilitating and executing the transactions that are part of the greater economy. In this role, marketers are expected to embrace the highest professional ethical norms and the ethical values implied by our responsibility toward multiple stakeholders (e.g., customers, employees, investors, peers, channel members, regulators and the host community).

Ethical Norms

As Marketers, we must:

1. **Do no harm**. This means consciously avoiding harmful actions or omissions by embodying high ethical standards and adhering to all applicable laws and regulations in the choices we make.

2. **Foster trust in the marketing system**. This means striving for good faith and fair dealing so as to contribute toward the efficacy of the exchange process as well as avoiding deception in product design, pricing, communication, and delivery of distribution.

3. **Embrace ethical values**. This means building relationships and enhancing consumer confidence in the integrity of marketing by affirming these core values: honesty, responsibility, fairness, respect, transparency and citizenship.

Ethical Values

Honesty—to be forthright in dealings with customers and stakeholders. To this end, we will:

- Strive to be truthful in all situations and at all times.

- Offer products of value that do what we claim in our communications.

- Stand behind our products if they fail to deliver their claimed benefits.

- Honor our explicit and implicit commitments and promises.

Responsibility—to accept the consequences of our marketing decisions and strategies. To this end, we will:

- Strive to serve the needs of customers.

- Avoid using coercion with all stakeholders.

- Acknowledge the social obligations to stakeholders that come with increased marketing and economic power.

- Recognize our special commitments to vulnerable market segments such as children, seniors, the economically impoverished, market illiterates and others who may be substantially disadvantaged.

- Consider environmental stewardship in our decision making.

Fairness—to balance justly the needs of the buyer with the interests of the seller. To this end, we will:

- Represent products in a clear way in selling, advertising and other forms of communication; this includes the avoidance of false, misleading and deceptive promotion.

- Reject manipulations and sales tactics that harm customer trust.

- Refuse to engage in price fixing, predatory pricing, price gouging or "bait-and-switch" tactics.

- Avoid knowing participation in conflicts of interest.

- Seek to protect the private information of customers, employees and partners.

Respect—to acknowledge the basic human dignity of all stakeholders. To this end, we will:

- Value individual differences and avoid stereotyping customers or depicting demographic groups (e.g., gender, race, sexual orientation) in a negative or dehumanizing way.

- Listen to the needs of customers and make all reasonable efforts to monitor and improve their satisfaction on an ongoing basis.

- Make every effort to understand and respectfully treat buyers, suppliers, intermediaries and distributors from all cultures.

- Acknowledge the contributions of others, such as consultants, employees and coworkers, to marketing endeavors.

- Treat everyone, including our competitors, as we would wish to be treated.

Transparency—to create a spirit of openness in marketing operations. To this end, we will:

- Strive to communicate clearly with all constituencies.

- Accept constructive criticism from customers and other stakeholders.

- Explain and take appropriate action regarding significant product or service risks, component substitutions or other foreseeable eventualities that could affect customers or their perception of the purchase decision.

- Disclose list prices and terms of financing as well as available price deals and adjustments.

Citizenship—to fulfill the economic, legal, philanthropic and societal responsibilities that serve stakeholders. To this end, we will:

- Strive to protect the ecological environment in the execution of marketing campaigns.

- Give back to the community through volunteerism and charitable donations.

- Contribute to the overall betterment of marketing and its reputation.

- Urge supply chain members to ensure that trade is fair for all participants, including producers in developing countries.

Implementation

We expect AMA members to be courageous and proactive in leading and/or aiding their organizations in the fulfillment of the explicit and implicit promises made to those stakeholders. We recognize that every industry sector and marketing sub-discipline (e.g., marketing research, e-commerce, Internet selling, direct marketing and advertising) has its own specific ethical issues that require policies and commentary. An array of such codes can be accessed through links on the AMA website. Consistent with the principle of subsidiarity (solving issues at the level where the expertise resides), we encourage all such groups to develop and/or refine their industry and discipline-specific codes of ethics to supplement these guiding ethical norms and values.

APPENDIX 4: INSTITUTE FOR ADVERTISING ETHICS

Preamble

The explosion of new technologies is changing the marketing and advertising landscape. New media, new ideas, new challenges are swirling around the industry and impacting the way it does business.

The one constant is transparency, and the need to conduct ourselves, our business, and our relationship with consumers in a fair, honest, and forthright manner.

This is especially true in today's often hostile environment, with revelations of wrong doing in particular industries and government programs resulting in an erosion of public confidence and trust in all our institutions.

It is particularly fitting in such times that we remind ourselves of the ethical behavior that should always guide our personal and business conduct.

The eight Principles and Practices presented here are the foundation on which the Institute for Advertising Ethics was created. They are based on the premise that all forms of communications, including advertising, should always do what is right for consumers, which in turn is right for business as well. For while we are in an age of unparalleled change, this overriding truth never changes.

Principles and Practices for Advertising Ethics

Principle 1—Advertising, public relations, marketing communications, news and editorial all share a common objective of truth and high ethical standards in serving the public.

Principle 2—Advertising, public relations, and all marketing communications professionals have an obligation to exercise the highest personal ethics in the creation and dissemination of commercial information to consumers.

Principle 3—Advertisers should clearly distinguish advertising, public relations and corporate communications from news and editorial content and entertainment, both online and offline.

Principle 4—Advertisers should clearly disclose all material conditions, such as payment or receipt of a free product, affecting endorsements in social and traditional channels, as well as the identity of endorsers, all in the interest of full disclosure and transparency.

Principle 5—Advertisers should treat consumers fairly based on the nature of the audience to whom the ads are directed and the nature of the product or service advertised.

Principle 6—Advertisers should never compromise consumers' personal privacy in marketing communications, and their choices as to whether to participate in providing their identity should be transparent and easily made.

Principle 7—Advertisers should follow federal, state and local laws, and cooperate with industry self-regulatory programs for the resolution of advertising practices.

Principle 8—Advertisers and their agencies, and online and offline media, should discuss privately potential ethical concerns, and members of the team creating ads should be given permission to express internally their ethical concerns.

APPENDIX 5: CHARTERED INSTITUTE OF PUBLIC RELATIONS CODE OF CONDUCT

Principles

1. Members of the Chartered Institute of Public Relations agree to:

   - Maintain the highest standards of professional endeavour, integrity, confidentiality, financial propriety and personal conduct;

   - Deal honestly and fairly in business with employers, employees, clients, fellow professionals, other professions and the public;

   - Respect the customs, practices and codes of clients, employers, colleagues, fellow professionals and other professions in all countries where they practise;

   - Take all reasonable care to ensure employment of best practice including giving no cause for Complaint of unfair discrimination on any grounds;

   - Work within the legal and regulatory frameworks affecting the practice of public relations in all countries where they practise;

   - Encourage professional training and development among Members of the profession;

   - Respect and abide by this Code and related Notes of Guidance issued by the Institute of Public Relations and encourage others to do the same.

Principles of Good Practice

2. Fundamental to good public relations practice are:

Integrity

   - Honest and responsible regard for the public interest;

   - Checking the reliability and accuracy of information before dissemination;

   - Never knowingly misleading clients, employers, employees, colleagues and fellow professionals about the nature of representation or what can be competently delivered and achieved;

   - Supporting the CIPR Principles by bringing to the attention of the CIPR examples of malpractice and unprofessional conduct.

Competence

   - Being aware of the limitations of professional competence: without limiting realistic scope for development, being willing to accept or delegate only that work for which practitioners are suitably skilled and experienced;

   - Where appropriate, collaborating on projects to ensure the necessary skill base.

Transparency and avoiding conflicts of interest

- Disclosing to employers, clients or potential clients any financial interest in a supplier being recommended or engaged;

- Declaring conflicts of interest (or circumstances which may give rise to them) in writing to clients, potential clients and employers as soon as they arise;

- Ensuring that services provided are costed and accounted for in a manner that conforms to accepted business practice and ethics.

Confidentiality

- Safeguarding the confidences of present and former clients and employers;

- Being careful to avoid using confidential and 'insider' information to the disadvantage or prejudice of clients and employers, or to self-advantage of any kind;

- Not disclosing confidential information unless specific permission has been granted or the public interest is at stake or if required by law.

Maintaining Professional Standards

3. CIPR Members are encouraged to spread awareness and pride in the public relations profession where practicable by, for example:

- Identifying and closing professional skills gaps through the Institute's Continuous Professional Development programme;

- Offering work experience to students interested in pursuing a career in public relations;

- Participating in the work of the Institute through the committee structure, special interest and vocational groups, training and networking events;

- Encouraging employees and colleagues to join and support the CIPR;

- Displaying the CIPR designatory letters on business stationery;

- Specifying a preference for CIPR applicants for staff positions advertised;

- Evaluating the practice of public relations through use of the CIPR Research & Evaluation Toolkit and other quality management and quality assurance systems (e.g., ISO standards); and constantly striving to improve the quality of business performance;

- Sharing information on good practice with Members and, equally, referring perceived examples of poor practice to the Institute.

Interpreting the Code

4. In the interpretation of this code, the Laws of the Land shall apply.

APPENDIX 6: THE IPRA CODE OF CONDUCT

Adopted in 2011 the IPRA Code of Conduct is an affirmation of professional and ethical conduct by members of the International Public Relations Association and recommended to public relations practitioners worldwide.

The Code consolidates the 1961 Code of Venice, the 1965 Code of Athens and the 2007 Code of Brussels.

a. *RECALLING the Charter of the United Nations which determines "to reaffirm faith in fundamental human rights, and in the dignity and worth of the human person";*

b. *RECALLING the 1948 "Universal Declaration of Human Rights" and especially recalling Article 19;*

c. *RECALLING that public relations, by fostering the free flow of information, contributes to the interests of all stakeholders;*

d. *RECALLING that the conduct of public relations and public affairs provides essential democratic representation to public authorities;*

e. *RECALLING that public relations practitioners through their wide-reaching communication skills possess a means of influence that should be restrained by the observance of a code of professional and ethical conduct;*

f. *RECALLING that channels of communication, such as the Internet and other digital media, are channels where erroneous or misleading information may be widely disseminated and remain unchallenged, and therefore demand special attention from public relations practitioners to maintain trust and credibility;*

g. *RECALLING that the Internet and other digital media demand special care with respect to the personal privacy of individuals, clients, employers and colleagues;*

In the conduct of public relations practitioners shall:

1. **Observance**

   Observe the principles of the UN Charter and the Universal Declaration of Human Rights;

2. **Integrity**

   Act with honesty and integrity at all times so as to secure and retain the confidence of those with whom the practitioner comes into contact;

3. **Dialogue**

   Seek to establish the moral, cultural and intellectual conditions for dialogue, and recognise the rights of all parties involved to state their case and express their views;

4. **Transparency**

   Be open and transparent in declaring their name, organisation and the interest they represent;

5. **Conflict**

   Avoid any professional conflicts of interest and disclose such conflicts to affected parties when they occur;

6. **Confidentiality**

   Honour confidential information provided to them;

7. **Accuracy**

   Take all reasonable steps to ensure the truth and accuracy of all information provided;

8. **Falsehood**

   Make every effort to not intentionally disseminate false or misleading information, exercise proper care to avoid doing so unintentionally and correct any such act promptly;

9. **Deception**

   Not obtain information by deceptive or dishonest means;

10. **Disclosure**

    Not create or use any organisation to serve an announced cause but which actually serves an undisclosed interest;

11. **Profit**

    Not sell for profit to third parties copies of documents obtained from public authorities;

12. **Remuneration**

    Whilst providing professional services, not accept any form of payment in connection with those services from anyone other than the principal;

13. **Inducement**

    Neither directly nor indirectly offer nor give any financial or other inducement to public representatives or the media, or other stakeholders;

14. **Influence**

    Neither propose nor undertake any action which would constitute an improper influence on public representatives, the media or other stakeholders;

15. **Competitors**

    Not intentionally injure the professional reputation of another practitioner;

16. **Poaching**

Not seek to secure another practitioner's client by deceptive means;

17. **Employment**

When employing personnel from public authorities or competitors take care to follow the rules and confidentiality requirements of those organisations;

18. **Colleagues**

Observe this Code with respect to fellow IPRA members and public relations practitioners worldwide.

IPRA members shall, in upholding this Code, agree to abide by and help enforce the disciplinary procedures of the International Public Relations Association in regard to any breach of this Code.

Adopted by the IPRA Board 5 November 2010

APPENDIX 7: THE PAGE PRINCIPLES

Arthur W. Page practiced seven principles of public relations management as a means of implementing his philosophy.

1. ***Tell the truth***. Let the public know what's happening and provide an accurate picture of the company's character, ideals and practices.

2. ***Prove it with action***. Public perception of an organization is determined 90 percent by what it does and 10 percent by what it says.

3. ***Listen to the customer***. To serve the company well, understand what the public wants and needs. Keep top decision makers and other employees informed about public reaction to company products, policies and practices.

4. ***Manage for tomorrow***. Anticipate public reaction and eliminate practices that create difficulties. Generate goodwill.

5. ***Conduct public relations as if the whole company depends on it***. Corporate relations is a management function. No corporate strategy should be implemented without considering its impact on the public. The public relations professional is a policymaker capable of handling a wide range of corporate communications activities.

6. ***Realize a company's true character is expressed by its people***. The strongest opinions—good or bad—about a company are shaped by the words and deeds of its employees. As a result, every employee—active or retired—is involved with public relations. It is the responsibility of corporate communications to support each employee's capability and desire to be an honest, knowledgeable ambassador to customers, friends, shareowners and public officials.

7. ***Remain calm, patient and good-humored***. Lay the groundwork for public relations miracles with consistent and reasoned attention to information and contacts. This may be difficult with today's contentious 24-hour news cycles and endless number of watchdog organizations. But when a crisis arises, remember, cool heads communicate best.

APPENDIX 8: SAMPLE PUBLIC RELATIONS PROPOSAL

Public Relations Plan for Golden Island Gourmet Jerky

March 26, 2012

Introduction

In response to the request for proposal from Golden Island Gourmet Snacks® for public relations services, the following is Morgan Marketing and Public Relations, LLC's analysis of the current public relations situation and our recommendations for developing and expanding the product market.

Golden Island Gourmet Jerky (Golden Island®) provides a worldly approach to beef and pork jerky in the United States, with more than 20 unique, culturally diverse flavors and a soft mouth-feel that is truly a treat for snack fans. Introduced into the marketplace via Costco roadshows in 2004, Golden Island is available at select Costco stores in 14 states and is ready to expand its market range. A proactive outreach will accomplish this goal.

The following is our analysis and recommendation for public relations and marketing for 2012. Our approach provides a multipronged and cost-effective method that capitalizes on Golden Island's strengths to expand its consumer market.

Situation Analysis

Political, Economic, Social, & Technological (PEST) Considerations

During this presidential election year, the United States is facing political uncertainty, both nationally and internationally. Gallup reports that Americans are divided on the trade-offs between energy production and environmental protection. Presidential approval decreases with age, ranging from 55% in the 18–29 demographic to 42% in Americans aged 65 or older. The economic outlook continues to be volatile, with American confidence increasing and decreasing from week to week.

Although discretionary income is still tight for many Americans, snack foods continue to sell well, and dried meat snack sales increased by 9.5% in 2011, according to the Snack Food Association. The Nielsen Company predicts that the meat snack sales will continue to grow, based on the 65% increase in 2008. Ad revenues on social media continue to grow, and Facebook is anticipated to reach $6.1 million, with Google running a close second.

Strengths, Weaknesses, Opportunities, & Threats (SWOT)

Strengths

- True and unique flavors (taste like bag label descriptions, a departure from other jerky brands)

- Low in sodium as compared to other brands of beef jerky

- High-protein, healthy snack

- Long history of culinary experience

- Soft mouth-feel, almost doesn't feel like you're eating jerky

- 100% made in the USA

- Minority and women-owned business

- Strong sales growth from 2009–2011 (more than 200%)

- Unique cooking processes, products are grilled and/or kettle cooked, unlike other jerky brands

- Eco-friendly packaging

- Appeals to both high-end and low-end consumers

- Certified to provide food products to the military

Weaknesses (Truly Opportunities)

- Lack of brand awareness

- In-person retail sales are limited, only at Costco and some online sales through the company website

- Lack of media coverage

- Lack of social media presence (Facebook/Golden Island Blog need to be updated frequently)

Opportunities

- Lack of gourmet jerky in the marketplace

- Facebook's new Timeline for Brands

- Snack food sales are growing (global sales are expected to reach $334.7 billion by 2015)

- Emerging trend of beef jerky as a gourmet product

Threats

- Krave Jerky, another "gourmet" product

- Reports against consumption of red meat

- Existing brand loyalty with largely known competitors (e.g., Jack's Links, Oberto, Blue Ox, all of which target athletes and men)

- Lingering negative connotation of jerky as "Bubba's snack"

Analysis

Golden Island has a unique product that is markedly different in flavor and mouthfeel from those of competitors. It is limited to in-person retail sales at Costco and some online sales through the company website, while 72% of jerky sales are through convenience stores (National Association of Convenience Stores). Clearly, jerky has not been treated as a gourmet snack, and negative images of the jerky products present minor obstacles to be overcome, while social media and Golden Island's certification to provide food to the military provide opportunities for additional market outreach.

Primary Research: A small local study supports secondary research findings. A brief questionnaire was posted to Facebook during the latter part of February and early March (see the Appendix for details on the survey). Most (74.2%) of the 120 respondents were aged 21–39, and the findings supported the information from our secondary sources. The survey yielded the following information:

- 94% of the participants indicated they did not know where Golden Island Jerky was sold.

- Respondents purchased jerky primarily at convenience stores, with grocery stores a distant second.

- The least favorite aspects of jerky was that it is:

  - Too chewy

  - Tough and hard to chew

- The top three qualities that respondents want in jerky are:

  - Flavor

  - Soft and tender

  - Price

- More than half (54%) consider jerky a good source of protein, but many do not consider it a healthful snack.

These findings indicate that Golden Island needs to reach a broader consumer base and that its unique mouth-feel positions it well for a favorable reception.

Problem Statement

Golden Island has lacked a full-scale entry into the consumer marketplace until now and wishes to expand its market reach. With a high-quality, unique product, Golden Island is well positioned to expand its market reach and overcome existing threats. The continued expansion of social media such as Facebook provides excellent opportunities to directly reach consumers, and military outreach can help introduce the product to new markets.

Target Audiences

The Nielsen Consumer Panel purchase data indicate that the traditional jerky consumer is a blue collar male, aged 35 to 54, earning $50,000–70,000 each year. However, current trends of focusing on nutritional value are expanding the consumer base, and jerky products are reflecting this expansion with a broader range of flavors, textures, and an emphasis on health.

We believe our core target audiences and areas for opportunity are:

- Men/Women ages 25–55

- Foodies to capitalize on the Golden Island as a gourmet product

- Athletes and outdoor enthusiasts to capitalize on jerky as a "packable, muscle-building snack" (BodyBuilding.com)

- Members of the military and their families

The Bureau of Labor Statistics reports that in 2010, nearly 11% of consumer food expenditures were for "miscellaneous foods," which includes snack foods. Our target public is composed of the 82,353,000 meat snack purchasers in the 25–55 age range. This means the psychographics and demographics are very broad, so media choices will reflect that breadth. In addition, 86% of global consumers, excluding the United Arab Emirates, believe that businesses should place equal weight on social and business interests, which places Golden Island's strong stance on social responsibility as an important asset.

The military and their families are prime targets for Golden Island Gourmet Jerky. While service members are on deployment, their families are seeking nonperishable products that can be easily sent in care packages. The Department of Defense reports that 97.9% of Marine Corps spouses are female, and most of them fit within our target age group. Donating to such military organizations as Marine Corps Family Readiness Offices will bring jerky directly to the target demographic, bolster the Golden Island image as a socially responsible organization, and potentially develop word-of-mouth marketing of the product.

Because of the portable nature of the product, athletes and outdoor enthusiasts are a logical target. Specific channels that reach each target are listed in tools and tactics below.

Influencers: "Foodies," both those identified by Moats Kennedy, Inc. as "health nuts" and "adventurous eaters," influence broader publics. This makes the foodie a prime target for promoting Golden Island Jerky as a gourmet product. According to a market research report on Reortbuyer.com, foodies are "avid, tech-savvy consumers who embrace all sorts of trends" and "introduce those trends to their communities and peers."

Business Goal

- Drive sales of Golden Island Gourmet Jerky and create first trial opportunities.

Positioning Statements

1. Position Golden Island as a brand that is constantly evolving.

2. Position Golden Island as an organization that is committed to actively giving back to its community.

3. Shift consumer perception of Golden Island jerky from a common snack to a gourmet treat.

Key Messages

1. Golden Island Jerky is a unique, gourmet product.

   - The products are prepared through grilling and kettle cooking processes.
   - The products have truly unusual flavors that reflect the descriptions on the bags.
   - The jerky has a soft mouth-feel, unlike that of other jerkies.

2. Golden Island Jerky is socially responsible.

   - The packaging is eco-friendly.
   - The company has a history of community engagement, such as the Holiday Giving Tree.

Campaign Identification

- **Made in America with Flavors from Around the World**

Objectives

1. **Create brand awareness of Golden Island products with at least 15 food distributors/buyers to increase in-store distribution of Golden Island Gourmet Jerky products by the end of the year.**

   Strategy: Showcase Golden Island's unique flavors, history, and story. Introduce the executive and sales team to the media and prospective distributors/buyers.

   Tactics: Creative writing and interviews.

   Tools: Create an informative press kit that updates existing documents and uses information gained from interviews and meetings with the president of Universal Food, the manufacturer of Golden Island Jerky Products, Anna Kan, and her colleagues Shelby Weeda, Tony Kan, Peter Shih, and Michael Kan to create the "Golden Island Voice/Theme." Documents will include:

   - Company overview
   - Fact sheet
   - Biographies and headshots of key Golden Island staff Anna Kan, Shelby Weeda, Rick McGuern, Tony Kan, Peter Shih, Mike Kan, and Laura Yamanaka
   - Golden Island Company milestones
   - Key messages/points of difference
   - Interesting jerky facts
   - Flavor description line sheet
   - Additional photos of jerky in the new Golden Island Test Kitchen

2. **Increase brand awareness of Golden Island by 10% with media and consumers on regional and national levels, as measured by pre- and postcampaign surveys.**

   Strategy: Highlight unique grilling and kettle cooking processes, flavors, and brand growth for placement in trade publications. Also highlight the environmentally friendly aspect of the master packaging that Golden Island products are sold in to gain additional coverage in eco-friendly/green media outlets.

   Tactics: Press releases, pitch letters, and media calls. These tactics will further Golden Island's message of unique flavors of beef and pork jerky and present them in a manner that will be well received by the media.

   Tools: Agency will proactively pitch publications such as:

   National Trade

   - Candy & Snack Today
   - Consumer Products Buyer, Grocery Headquarters
   - Convenience Store News
   - Meat & Poultry Magazine
   - National Provisioner
   - Independent Processor

- Snack Food & Wholesale Bakery
- Specialty Food Magazine
- The Gourmet Retailer
- On-Campus Hospitality
- Campus Dining Today

National and Regional Businesses

- Forbes
- Forbes Small Business
- Entrepreneur
- Fortune
- Inland Empire Business Journal
- Press Enterprise

Women-Owned Business Publications

- Professional Women's Business Magazine
- Little PINK Book/Pink Magazine
- Professional Women's Magazine
- Working Mother Magazine
- Enterprising Women Magazine
- Diversity Woman Magazine
- Enterprising Women Magazine
- Women Entrepreneurs
- Working Woman

Minority Publications

- Diversity Executive
- Minority Business Entrepreneur Magazine
- Diversityinc.com
- Agency will monitor editorial calendars of publications for other opportunities

Asian Publications

- Asian-Pacific publications

Christian Publications

- Christianity Today
- Christian Woman

Additionally, in regard to the eco-friendly packaging, the agency will proactively pitch the following outlets:

- April issues of many publications (Earth Day is in April, lots of "green" stories)
- Greener Package Magazine
- The Packaging Professional
- Packaging Digest
- Packaging World

As with the trade media, we will reach out in a similar fashion to consumer outlets such as food and snack magazines and publications targeted to outdoor and sports enthusiasts, highlighting the unique qualities of Golden Island Gourmet Jerky, such as the health benefits of jerky, cooking process, flavors, and softness as compared to other brands of jerky.

Morgan Marketing's outreach in these markets will consist of food, snack, and business editors at the major newspapers, food and family bloggers, and food-focused television media for the markets in which Golden Island is currently selling. (Additional markets will follow as distribution expands.)

National Consumer, Food

- Bon Appetit
- Chow
- Delish.com
- Epicurious
- Food & Wine
- Relish
- Wall Street Journal Weekend Edition
- Influential Bloggers
- Cooking with Paula Deen
- The Food Network Magazine

National Consumer, Television

- The Rachael Ray Show
- The Martha Stewart Show
- Guy's Big Bite
- The Chew
- The Ellen DeGeneres Show
- The Food Network

National Consumer, Women's Interest

- O, The Oprah Magazine
- EveryDay with Rachael Ray

- Martha Stewart Living
- Good Housekeeping
- Sunset Magazine

National Consumer, Outdoor/Sports Enthusiasts

- Men's Health
- Backpacker
- American Hunter
- Field and Stream
- Outdoor Life
- Outside
- Outside's Go Magazine
- BackpackingLight.com
- Natural Muscle Magazine
- Women's Health Magazine
- Ironman Magazine

National Consumer, Travel Publications

- Los Angeles Times Travel Section
- Orange County Register Travel Section
- Traveling magazines/publications
- Travel bloggers
- Departures
- Condé Nast Traveler
- Condé Nast Travel+Leisure
- Westways
- Good Sam Club, Highways Magazine

National Consumer, In-Flight

- Southwest Airlines, Spirit Magazine
- American Airlines, American Way Magazine
- Delta Airlines, Delta Sky Magazine
- Hemispheres Magazine
- SkyMall Magazine (An Advertising Vehicle)

Markets Surrounding Costco/Central Market Locations

- Los Angeles/Orange County/Inland Empire
- Northern California

- Connecticut

- Delaware

- Hawaii

- Maryland

- Massachusetts

- Nevada

- New Hampshire

- New York

- Pennsylvania

- Texas

- Vermont

- Virginia

- Food and Family bloggers in each market

- Costco Connection

The press kit will be the starting point for Golden Island's voice and messaging. With a unique and long family history, Golden Island has a great story to tell and the press kit will set the theme and tone for that message. The press kit will also make the company human through the biographies of company leadership. Our messaging and theme for Golden Island will revolve around the phrase *Made in America with Flavors from Around the World*, which adds to the mystique and flavor adventure consumers experience when eating Golden Island products. This is a message that will resonate well with many jerky buyers, eaters, and the media.

3. **By the end of the year, expand the current distributor and buyer marketing program by 10% percent.**

   Strategy: Client will identify pertinent food distributors and buyers across the country and introduce the Golden Island brand and products to them, setting the stage for meetings with the Golden Island sales team.

   Tactics: Agency will create an attractive brochure and an innovative mailer campaign geared to distributors/buyers with percentages of sales figures and reasons to stock Golden Island products. The mailer will be performed in a two-step process.

   1. Send a creative pitch press release about the new and attractive packaging and announcing the new website.

   2. Send samples of products for distributors and buyers to taste again with a creative pitch letter.

4. **Develop a social media presence for Golden Island by the end of the year.**

   Media have transformed in recent years with the success of social media platforms such as Facebook, Twitter, and Pinterest. It is something that is no longer a consideration but a mandatory tool in the field of public relations.

Strategy: Place pictures of jerky products and inspiration for jerky such as marinades, smokehouses, or even creative ways people are enjoying beef jerky, i.e., Bloody Marys, salads, while on trips, etc.

Tactics: Expand social media presence through a website and Facebook overhaul with regular postings on Facebook and on the Golden Island blog and the addition of a Twitter handle and Pinterest.

Tools: Agency will draft a weekly Facebook posting sheet with 5–10 engaging posts per week. These posts will not be solely about Golden Island but rather a variety of topics that interest the jerky eater, such as sports, outdoor activities, etc.

Since March 30, 2012, Facebook has required all brands to follow the "Timeline" format. This change allows the Golden Island page to have a large image as its "Background" and also gives the brand a chance to expand its history beyond the time it has had a Facebook presence going back as far as the company's roots in Taiwan in 1952.

Agency will also provide information to client about Facebook advertising, which can grow brand followers and the base of customers connected via social media.

With the client's input, the agency will also draft and edit regular postings to the Golden Island blog. These weekly posts will be a longer version of a topic discussed during the week in a Facebook post.

The agency will create five twitter postings per week, which are short and designed to generate excitement with the brand.

Pinterest is the latest social media outlet to gain considerable notoriety. It is a visual medium that focuses on pictures placed on a virtual "pin board" where users can post images of items they find of interest on the Internet.

The agency will create a Golden Island pin board and send the client 10 photos gained from research online and any copy that should accompany the photos for approval.

5. **Develop brand loyalty and a Golden Island following among military and military families by the end of the year.**

   Strategy: Partner with military support groups to establish a positive relationship with this target public.

   Tactics: Agency will research and contact SoCal [Southern California] military bases and military unit family support groups to donate Golden Island product for care packages. The agency will also contact the City of Rancho Cucamonga, as it has a long history of military support and the local connection between the Kans and Golden Island's place of business is a natural fit. Additionally, the agency will look into opportunities to work with groups such as the Wounded Warrior project.

   Tools: Once a group is identified and Golden Island has begun supporting them, the agency will contact military publications to bring awareness of the work and support Golden Island is giving the troops and will also work toward gaining product reviews in the publications. Further media relations work will involve contacting Sean Hannity of Fox News, who has helped the Wounded Warrior project in years past. All efforts will be subjects for posts on Golden Island's website and social media platforms.

Military publications include

- Military Living
- Military Magazine
- Stars and Stripes
- The Leatherneck
- Marine Times
- Soldier's Magazine
- Navy Times

6. **Enhance the brand's image by highlighting the company's philanthropic efforts.**

   Strategy: Golden Island has a distinct focus on the wellbeing of its employees and their communities. Projects such as the Holiday Giving Tree and the efforts to better the lives of those in the surrounding communities are a rarity in business and should be touted.

   Tactics: The agency will use media pitch letters, press releases, and follow-up calls to human interest editors and reporters in the communities where the Golden Island philanthropic efforts are taking place. These philanthropic efforts and media gained from the outreach about philanthropy will also be promoted on Golden Island's social media platforms and website.

7. **Position Anna Kan as an expert in business and leadership for speaking engagements, gaining exposure for her and the Golden Island Brand.**

   Strategy: With Anna Kan's experience in corporate leadership and devotion to helping people better themselves and her community, she is a perfect fit for speaking engagements to aspiring entrepreneurs, as well as undergraduate and graduate degree students who wish to start their own businesses.

   Tactics: Agency will research speaking engagements in the Inland Empire and surrounding area with Asian, women, and business groups where Anna Kan can attend and speak on her experiences, inspiring others to follow their dreams and callings. This will allow another outlet for Anna Kan to give back to the community while building greater brand recognition for Golden Island.

   Tools: Possible speaking engagement opportunities:

   - USC Marshall School of Business, Lloyd Greif Center for Entrepreneurial Studies
   - Entrepreneurship groups
   - University of California, Riverside Anderson Graduate School of Management
   - CSU, Fullerton Mihaylo College of Business and Economics, Center for Entrepreneurship
   - IE area Chambers of Commerce

8. **Possible 2013 Objective: Position Golden Island Jerky as a true gourmet chef's product.**

   Strategy: Have high-profile chefs cook with Golden Island jerky to gain notoriety as a truly gourmet product.

   Tactics: The agency will research chefs already using jerky and contact them via pitch letters and product samples. The agency will follow up with these chefs to see if they are interested in switching to Golden Island jerky in place of the products they are currently using. If successful, the agency will publicize chefs using Golden Island products in the markets where the chefs live and work.

9. **Possible 2013 Objective: Position Golden Island as a leader in the industry and local community through award recognition.**

   Strategy: In building Golden Island's public relations presence, the agency will actively research and pursue award opportunities, which will bring greater exposure to the brand and its efforts to not only sell jerky but also take an active interest in the wellbeing of employees and their families.

   Tactics: The agency will research award opportunities in both snack trade and the Inland Empire and present to client prior to entering. If Golden Island wins the award competitions entered, the agency will produce and distribute press releases and promote the award recognition on Golden Island's social media platforms and website which will bring greater awareness to the Golden Island brand and its status as a leader in the meat snack industry and Inland Empire community.

Campaign Timeline

March: Create media list and identify editorial calendar opportunities.

April: Draft and finalize press kit.

April: Agency will finalize distributor and buyer marketing program and begin distributing information.

May: Agency will begin social media postings and will launch Twitter and Pinterest pages.

May: Agency will identify list of award opportunities and discuss which to enter with client and timeline of entry deadlines.

May: Agency will research speaking engagements and present to client.

May: Finalize product release (specific product or products TBD) and distribute to trade and consumer media; agency will pitch for an entire month after distribution of release.

August: Develop 2013 PR plan.

September: Agency will present research on which local military units to donate Golden Island product.

October: Agency will contact military media to pitch story about donations to military unit.

November: Agency will contact media regarding Golden Island philanthropic efforts with a holiday push and pitch surrounding the company's giving tree.

: Campaign Timeline Gantt Chart

Activity	Mar	Apr	May	Jun	Jul	Aug	Sep	Oct	Nov	Dec
Create media list	■									
Identify editorial calendar opportunities	■									
Draft and finalize press release		■								
Finalize distributor & buyer marketing program		■								
Begin distributing information			■							
Identify & dicuss list of award opportunities			■							
Research & present speaking opportunities to client			■							
Finalize product release			■							
Distribute product release to trade & consumer media			■							
Agency pitches all month				■						
Develop 2013 plan						■				
Present research on local military units to receive donations							■			
Contact military media								■		
Contact media re: philanthropy with holiday push									■	
Pitch Giving Tree									■	

APPENDIX TABLE 8-1: Campaign Budget

Direct Program Costs	Jan	Feb	Mar	Apr	May	Jun	Totals
Research							
Books (specify titles)	$350						$350
Dues & Subscriptions (specify)	$200						$200
Focus Groups		$2,500					$2,500
Pre-Post Campaign Surveys	$1,250	$0	$0	$0	$0	$1,250	$2,500
Subtotal	*$1,800*	*$2,500*	*$0*	*$0*	*$0*	*$1,250*	*$5,550*
Publicity							
Press Kits	$0	$0	$1,275	$0	$0	$0	$1,275
Mailing Supplies & Postage	$0	$0	$1,200	$0	$0	$0	$1,200
Distribution Service (specify)	$0	$0	$800	$0	$0	$0	$800
Media Monitoring & Clipping Service	$0	$0	$700	$700	$700	$700	$2,800
Printing & Folding × 1,000	$0	$1,500	$0	$0	$0	$0	$1,500
Subtotal	*$0*	*$1,500*	*$3,975*	*$700*	*$700*	*$700*	*$7,575*
Program Total	**$1,800**	**$4,000**	**$3,975**	**$700**	**$700**	**$1,950**	**$13,125**

Campaign Budget

NOTE: The budget for this plan is proprietary, so the information in Table 8-1 is a partial hypothetical example of a budget format.

Evaluation

1. The first objective, which is to create brand awareness of Golden Island products with at least 15 food distributors/buyers, will be evaluated by counting the number of distributors/buyers that have accepted the product. In-store distribution of Golden Island Gourmet Jerky products will be assessed by tracking the products distributed and the stores in which distribution took place.

2. The objective to increase brand awareness of Golden Island by 10% with media and consumers on regional and national levels, will be measured by pre- and postcampaign surveys.

3. The objective to expand the current distributor and buyer marketing program by 10% will be evaluated by comparing precampaign figures with postcampaign figures.

4. The objective to develop a social media presence for Golden Island by the end of the year will be evaluated by such tracking such things as Facebook "likes," followers, fans, and online comments from the community.

5. The objective to develop brand loyalty and a Golden Island following among military and military families by the end of the year will be evaluated by tracking the number of military support groups that partner with Golden Island and sales at military installations.

6. The objective to enhance the brand's image by highlighting the company's philanthropic efforts will be measured by pre- and postcampaign attitudinal surveys.

7. The objective to position Anna Kan as an expert in business and leadership for speaking engagements, gaining exposure for her and the Golden Island Brand will be evaluated by the number of speaking engagements completed and informal feedback from the audiences.

The Team

At Morgan Marketing & PR, we have small teams of very smart people giving a great deal of concentration to our clients. Every client matters, and our service reflects that. Clients partner with experienced practitioners, not entry level staff, and our long-term client relationships speak to the success we achieve. Our services are delivered by friendly, focused professionals with strong values and insightful ideas. And, with a specialty in the food and restaurant industry, all our clients benefit from our onsite test kitchen (who doesn't like warm, homemade chocolate chips cookies at their meetings?).

Melinda Morgan
Kartsonis, APR,
Fellow PRSA —
*President,
Agency Principal*

Photo © Lovàto Images

Spend 10 minutes with Melinda Morgan Kartsonis and you'll realize why Morgan Marketing has achieved the success it enjoys today. Sitting at the helm, she leads the charge in building an agency that fosters creativity, communication, and energy. From her personal design of the open offices, to the cheerleader roles she takes with her staff, to her hands-on approach in creativity, it's no wonder she is viewed as passionate, encouraging, and straightforward.

Beginning more than 25 years ago working for a prestigious Michigan Avenue PR firm in Chicago, she spent the 1980s honing her craft working for various agencies. Melinda moved on to open Morgan Marketing & PR in 1991. Combining her attention to detail, her ability to develop relationships, and her aggressive, results-oriented approach to marketing communications, she has quickly built a client roster to be proud of.

Melinda has always been active in the community, with an impressive list of board or committee positions for organizations such as City of Hope, St. Joseph Hospital, Orange County Performing Arts Center Business Partnership Alliance, California Restaurant Association of Orange County, American Institute of Wine and Food, the American Cancer Society Corporate Advisory Council, Women's Foodservice Forum, and Les Dames d'Escoffier International. To share her passion for the PR industry, she has also been a faculty member at University of California at Irvine, Chapman

University, California State University Fullerton, and California State University Long Beach, and she's served with the Orange County Public Relations Society of America.

She's received the Public Relations Society of America Distinguished Service Award, been included with *Orange Coast* magazine's "Hot 11" in its Power of PR issue, and been named the Orange County's *Business Journal's* "Top Businesswoman"— many times. She has also received awards from the Cystic Fibrosis Foundation (Orange County's Finest) and American Lung Association (Volunteer of the Year).

So what makes Melinda tick? She requires Think Tank time—quiet time alone behind the wheel of her car formulating the next big splash.

A Southern California native, Stephen lives by the mantra Work Hard, Play Hard. With a wealth of experience exclusively in agency public relations, Stephen thrives in the fast-paced world of managing multiple clients, meeting critical deadlines, and developing media placements. At Morgan Marketing and Public Relations, LLC, Stephen is responsible for the day-to-day needs of a number of clients, which include strategic planning, implementing communications programs, crafting press releases and collateral materials, pitching stories to a variety of media outlets, fulfilling the social media needs of clients, as well as facilitating the growth of new business.

Stephen Gregg, Senior Account Executive

Photo © Tom Duncan

Prior to joining the team at Morgan Marketing and Public Relations, LLC, Stephen served with Faubel Public Affairs and represented both private companies and public agencies, working on numerous community outreach campaigns throughout Orange County, California. Notably, he led the communications campaign for the victorious "Yes on Measure B" project in San Juan Capistrano, which upheld a city council's decision on property rights. Stephen also has a wealth of experience representing clients in the areas of healthcare, consumer products, architecture, and entertainment.

When Stephen is not in the office, he enjoys traveling, working on his vintage Mustang, and experimenting in the kitchen. He is an Eagle Scout, an avid beachgoer, snowboarder, and outdoorsman.

Stephen is also active as a volunteer with Future Leaders of Our Community, and he is a member of the Public Relations Society of America. He graduated from California State University, Fullerton, with a Bachelor of Arts degree in Communications: Public Relations, and lives in Laguna Niguel.

Appendices

Primary Research Methods

A link to a questionnaire was posted to Facebook, yielding 120 responses. The questionnaire was composed of the following items:

Open-Ended Questions

1. What is your least favorite thing about jerky?

2. What is your favorite characteristic of jerky?

3. What qualities do you want in jerky?

The responses were tabulated into categories. The most popular two or three are reported in the proposal.

Closed-Ended Questions

1. Do you take jerky with you on the go?   Yes   No

2. Is jerky a good source of protein?   Yes   No

3. Have you heard of Golden Island Jerky? Yes   No

4. Where do you purchase jerky?

    a. Costco

    b. Convenience stores

    c. Markets

    d. Other

5. What are your reasons for eating jerky?

    a. Taste

    b. Convenience

    c. Nutrition

    d. Other

6. What is your gender?   Male   Female

    What is your age?   18–24   25–39   40–59   60+

References

Agricultural Marketing Resource Center. (2012). *Dried beef industry profile.* Ames, IA: Author. Retrieved from http://www.agmrc.org/commodities__products/livestock/beef/dried_beef_industry_profile.cfm

Clark, S. (2011, March 22). *12 packable muscle-building snacks.* Meridian, ID: BodyBuilding.com. Retrieved from http://www.bodybuilding.com/fun/12-packable-muscle-building-snacks.html

Fredricksen, C. (2012, February 22). *Google edges closer to Facebook as U.S. display advertising becomes two-horse race* [Press release]. New York: eMarketer. Retrieved from http://www.emarketer.com/PressRelease.aspx?R=1008856

Gallup. (2012, March 12–18). *Gallup daily: Politics* [Poll]. Washington, DC: Author. Retrieved from http://www.gallup.com/poll/politics.aspx

Gallup. (2012, March 12–18). *Gallup economy* [Poll]. Washington, DC: Author. Retrieved from http://www.gallup.com/poll/economy.aspx.

Global Industry Analysts, Inc. (2012, January 18). *Global snack foods market to reach US$334.7 by 2015, according to new report by Global Industry Analysts, Inc.* Retrieved from http://www.prweb.com/releases/snack_foods_nut_snacks/microwaveable_snacks/prweb9116978.htm

Goodpurpose. (2010). *The Goodpurpose 4th annual global study.* Retrieved from http://www.goodpurposecommunity.com/pages/globalstudy.aspx#

Kowalski, A., & Chandra, S. (2012). U.S. outlook optimism at eight-year high: Economy. *Bloomberg Businessweek: NewsFromBloomberg.* Retrieved from http://www.businessweek.com/news/2012-03-22/jobless-claims-in-u-dot-s-dot-decline-to-lowest-level-in-four-years

Moats Kennedy, Inc. (2011, October 3). *Demographics: Foodies take a new turn.* Chicago: Author. Retrieved from http://www.moatskennedy.com/2011/10/03/demographics-foodies-take-a-new-turn

Report Buyer. (2009, January). *Foodies in the U.S.: Five cohorts: Foreign/spicy, restaurant, cooks, gourmet and organic/natural* [Market research report]. London: Author. Retrieved from http://www.reportbuyer.com/leisure_media/dining/foodies_u_s_five_cohorts_foreign_spicy_restaurant_cooks_gourmet_organic_natural.html

Schaefer, R. (2012). *Beef jerky manufacturing* [Nielsen consumer panel]. San Antonio: SBDCNet. Retrieved from http://www.sbdcnet.org/small-business-research-reports/beef-jerky-manufacturing

Snack Food Association. (2012, March 16). *The snack report—March 16, 2012.* Arlington, VA: Author. Retrieved from http://www.sfa2.org/news.php?id=62

U.S. Department of Defense. (2010). *Demographics 2010: Profile of the military community.* Washington, DC: Author. Retrieved from http://www.militaryhomefront.dod.mil/12038/Project%20Documents/MilitaryHOMEFRONT/Reports/2010_Demographics_Report.pdf

APPENDIX 9 ANNOTATED PUBLIC RELATIONS PROPOSAL

I. Introduction

A. **Brief background of the client organization.**

Golden Island Gourmet Jerky (Golden Island®) provides a worldly approach to beef and pork jerky in the United States with more than 20 unique, culturally diverse flavors and a soft mouth-feel that is truly a treat for snack fans.

B. **Description of who is offering the proposal and why.**

In response to the request for proposal from Golden Island Gourmet Snacks® for public relations services, the following is Morgan Marketing and Public Relations, LLC's analysis of the current public relations situation and our recommendations for developing and expanding the product market.

C. **Overview of the problems and potential solutions.**

Introduced into the marketplace via Costco roadshows in 2004, Golden Island is available at select Costco stores in 14 states and is ready to expand its market range. A proactive outreach will accomplish this goal.

D. **Rationale for public relations as a cost-effective approach to the problem.**

The following is our analysis and recommendation for public relations and marketing for 2012. Our approach provides a multipronged and cost-effective method that capitalizes on Golden Island's strengths to expand its consumer market.

II. Problem Statement

A. **Research**

1. **Situation Analysis**

   a. **Political, Economic, Social, and Technological Issues faced by the client (PEST Analysis).**

   During this presidential election year, the United States is facing political uncertainty, both nationally and internationally. Gallup reports that Americans are divided on the trade-offs between energy production and environmental protection. Presidential approval decreases with age, ranging from 55% in the 18–29 demographic to 42% in Americans aged 65 or older. The economic outlook continues to be volatile, with American confidence increasing and decreasing from week to week.

   Although discretionary income is still tight for many Americans, snack foods continue to sell well, and dried meat snack sales increased by 9.5% in 2011, according to the Snack Food Association. The Nielsen

Company predicts that the meat snack sales will continue to grow, based on the 65% increase in 2008. Ad revenues on social media continue to grow, and Facebook is anticipated to reach $6.1 million, with Google running a close second.

b. **Client Strengths, Weaknesses, Opportunities, and Threats (SWOT Analysis)**

Strengths

- True and unique flavors (taste like bag label descriptions, a departure from other jerky brands)
- Low in sodium as compared to other brands of beef jerky
- High-protein, healthy snack
- Long history of culinary experience
- Soft mouth-feel, almost doesn't feel like you're eating jerky
- 100% made in the USA
- Minority and Women-Owned Business
- Strong sales growth from 2009–2011 (more than 200%)
- Unique cooking processes; products are grilled and/or kettle cooked, unlike other jerky brands
- Eco-friendly packaging
- Appeals to both high-end and low-end consumers
- Certified to provide food products to the military

Weaknesses (Truly Opportunities)

- Lack of brand awareness
- In-person retail sales are limited; only at Costco and some online sales through the company website
- Lack of media coverage
- Lack of social media presence (Facebook/Golden Island Blog need to be updated frequently)

Opportunities

- Lack of gourmet jerky in the marketplace
- Facebook's new Timeline for Brands
- Snack food sales are growing (global sales are expected to reach $334.7 billion by 2015)
- Emerging trend of beef jerky as a gourmet product

Threats

- Krave Jerky, another "gourmet" product

- Reports against consumption of red meat

- Existing brand loyalty with largely known competitors (e.g., Jack's Links, Oberto, Blue Ox, all of which target athletes and men)

- Lingering negative connotation of jerky as "Bubba's snack"

Analysis

Golden Island has a unique product that is markedly different in flavor and mouth-feel from those of its competitors. It is limited to in-person retail sales at Costco and some online sales through the company website, while 72% of jerky sales are through convenience stores (National Association of Convenience Stores). Clearly, jerky has not been treated as a gourmet snack, and negative images of the jerky products present minor obstacles to be overcome, while social media and Golden Island's certification to provide food to the military provide opportunities for additional market outreach.

Primary Research: A small local study supports secondary research findings. A brief questionnaire was posted to Facebook during the latter part of February and early March (see the Appendix for details on the survey). Most (74.2%) of the 120 respondents were aged 21–39, and the findings supported the information from our secondary sources. The survey yielded the following information:

- 94% of the participants indicated they did not know where Golden Island Jerky was sold.

- Respondents purchased jerky primarily at convenience stores, with grocery stores a distant second.

- The least favorite aspects of jerky was that it is

  - Too chewy

  - Tough and hard to chew

- The top three qualities that respondents want in jerky are:

  - Flavor

  - Soft and tender

  - Price

- More than half (54%) consider jerky a good source of protein, but many do not consider it a healthful snack.

These findings indicate that Golden Island needs to reach a broader consumer base and that its unique mouth-feel positions it well for a favorable reception.

c. **Problem Statement**

Golden Island has lacked a full-scale entry into the consumer market-place until now and wishes to expand its market reach. With a high-quality, unique product, Golden Island is well positioned to expand its market reach and overcome existing threats. The continued expansion of social media such as Facebook provides excellent opportunities to directly reach consumers, and military outreach can help introduce the product to new markets.

2. **Analysis of Key Publics**

Target Audiences

The Nielsen Consumer Panel purchase data indicate that the traditional jerky consumer is a blue collar male, aged 35 to 54, earning $50,000–70,000 each year. However, current trends of focusing on nutritional value are expanding the consumer base, and jerky products are reflecting this expansion with a broader range of flavors, textures, and an emphasis on health.

We believe our core target audiences and areas for opportunity are:

- Men/Women ages 25–55

- Foodies to capitalize on the Golden Island as a gourmet product

- Athletes and outdoor enthusiasts to capitalize on jerky as a "packable, muscle-building snack" (BodyBuilding.com)

- Members of the military and their families

The Bureau of Labor Statistics reports that in 2010, nearly 11% of consumer food expenditures were for "miscellaneous foods," which includes snack foods. Our target public is composed of the 82,353,000 meat snack purchasers in the 25–55 age range. This means the psychographics and demographics are very broad, so media choices will reflect that breadth. In addition, 86% of global consumers, excluding the United Arab Emirates, believe that businesses should place equal weight on social and business interests, which places Golden Island's strong stance on social responsibility as an important asset.

The military and their families are prime targets for Golden Island Gourmet Jerky. While service members are on deployment, their families are seeking nonperishable products that can be easily sent in care packages. The Department of Defense reports that 97.9% of Marine Corps spouses are female, and most of them fit within our target age group. Donating to such military organizations as Marine Corps Family Readiness Offices will bring jerky directly to the target demographic, bolster the Golden Island image as a socially responsible organization, and potentially develop word-of-mouth marketing of the product.

Because of the portable nature of the product, athletes and outdoor enthusiasts are a logical target. Specific channels that reach each target are listed in tools and tactics below.

Influencers: "Foodies," both those identified by Moats Kennedy, Inc. as "health nuts" and "adventurous eaters," influence broader publics. This makes the foodie a prime target for promoting Golden Island Jerky as a gourmet product. According to a market research report on Reortbuyer.com, foodies are "avid, tech-savvy consumers who embrace all sorts of trends" and "introduce those trends to their communities and peers."

II. WORK STATEMENT

A. **Planning**

1. **Goals & SMART Objectives**

Business Goal

- Drive sales of Golden Island Gourmet Jerky and create first trial opportunities.

Positioning Statements

- Position Golden Island as a brand that is constantly evolving.

- Position Golden Island as an organization that is committed to actively giving back to its community.

- Shift consumer perception of Golden Island jerky from a common snack to a gourmet treat.

Objectives

1. Create brand awareness of Golden Island products with at least 15 food distributors/buyers to increase in-store distribution of Golden Island Gourmet Jerky products by the end of the year.

2. Increase brand awareness of Golden Island by 10% with media and consumers on regional and national levels, as measured by pre- and postcampaign surveys.

3. By the end of the year, expand the current distributor and buyer marketing program by 10%.

4. Develop a social media presence for Golden Island by the end of the year.

5. Develop brand loyalty and a Golden Island following among military and military families by the end of the year

6. Enhance the brand's image by highlighting the company's philanthropic efforts.

7. Position Anna Kan as an expert in business and leadership for speaking engagements, gaining exposure for her and the Golden Island Brand.

8. Possible 2013 Objective: Position Golden Island Jerky as a true gourmet chef's product.

9. Possible 2013 Objective: Position Golden Island as a leader in the industry and local community through award recognition.

2. Key Messages

Key Messages

- Golden Island Jerky is a unique, gourmet product.

  - The products are prepared through grilling and kettle cooking processes.

  - The products have truly unusual flavors that reflect the descriptions on the bags.

  - The jerky has a soft mouth-feel, unlike that of other jerkies.

- Golden Island Jerky is socially responsible.

  - The packaging is eco-friendly.

  - The company has a history of community engagement, such as the Holiday Giving Tree.

Campaign Identification

- **Made in America with Flavors from Around the World**

B. Implementation

1. **Strategy**: Showcase Golden Island's unique flavors, history, and story. Introduce the executive and sales team to the media and prospective distributors/buyers.

   Tactics: Creative writing and interviews

   Tools: Create an informative press kit that updates existing documents and uses information gained from interviews and meetings with the president of Universal Food, the manufacturer of Golden Island Jerky Products, Anna Kan, and her colleagues Shelby Weeda, Tony Kan, Peter Shih, and Michael Kan to create the "Golden Island Voice/Theme." Documents will include:

   - Company overview
   - Fact sheet
   - Biographies and headshots of key Golden Island staff: Anna Kan, Shelby Weeda, Rick McGuern, Tony Kan, Peter Shih, Mike Kan, and Laura Yamanaka
   - Golden Island Company milestones
   - Key messages/points of difference
   - Interesting jerky facts
   - Flavor description line sheet
   - Additional photos of jerky in the new Golden Island test kitchen

2. **Strategy**: Highlight unique grilling and kettle cooking processes, flavors, and brand growth for placement in trade publications. Also highlight the environmentally friendly aspect of the master packaging that Golden Island products are sold in to gain additional coverage in eco-friendly/green media outlets.

Tactics: Press releases, pitch letters, and media calls. These tactics will further Golden Island's message of unique flavors of beef and pork jerky and present them in a manner that will be well received by the media.

Tools: Agency will proactively pitch publications such as:

National Trade

- Candy & Snack Today
- Consumer Products Buyer, Grocery Headquarters
- Convenience Store News
- Meat & Poultry Magazine
- National Provisioner
- Independent Processor
- Snack Food & Wholesale Bakery
- Specialty Food Magazine
- The Gourmet Retailer
- On-Campus Hospitality
- Campus Dining Today

National and Regional Businesses

- Forbes
- Forbes Small Business
- Entrepreneur
- Fortune
- Inland Empire Business Journal
- Press Enterprise

Women-Owned Business Publications

- Professional Women's Business Magazine
- Little PINK Book/Pink Magazine
- Professional Women's Magazine
- Working Mother Magazine
- Enterprising Women Magazine
- Diversity Woman Magazine

- Enterprising Women Magazine
- Women Entrepreneurs
- Working Woman

Minority Publications

- Diversity Executive
- Minority Business Entrepreneur Magazine
- Diversityinc.com
- Agency will monitor editorial calendars of publications for other opportunities

Asian Publications

- Asian-Pacific publications

Christian Publications

- Christianity Today
- Christian Woman

Additionally, in regard to the eco-friendly packaging, the agency will pro-actively pitch the following outlets:

- April issues of many publications (Earth Day is in April, lots of "green" stories)
- Greener Package Magazine
- The Packaging Professional
- Packaging Digest
- Packaging World

As with the trade media, we will reach out in a similar fashion to consumer outlets, such as food and snack magazines and publications targeted to outdoor and sports enthusiasts, highlighting the unique qualities of Golden Island Gourmet Jerky, such as the health benefits of jerky, cooking process, flavors, and softness as compared to other brands of jerky.

Morgan Marketing's outreach in these markets will consist of food, snack, and business editors at the major newspapers, food and family bloggers, and food-focused television media for the markets in which Golden Island is currently selling. (Additional markets will follow as distribution expands.)

National Consumer, Food

- Bon Appetit
- Chow
- Delish.com

- Epicurious
- Food & Wine
- Relish
- Wall Street Journal Weekend Edition
- Influential Bloggers
- Cooking with Paula Deen
- The Food Network Magazine

National Consumer, Television

- The Rachael Ray Show
- The Martha Stewart Show
- Guy's Big Bite
- The Chew
- The Ellen DeGeneres Show
- The Food Network

National Consumer, Women's Interest

- O, The Oprah Magazine
- EveryDay with Rachael Ray
- Martha Stewart Living
- Good Housekeeping
- Sunset Magazine

National Consumer, Outdoor/Sports Enthusiasts

- Men's Health
- Backpacker
- American Hunter
- Field and Stream
- Outdoor Life
- Outside
- Outside's Go Magazine
- BackpackingLight.com
- Natural Muscle Magazine
- Women's Health Magazine
- Ironman Magazine

National Consumer, Travel Publications

- Los Angeles Times Travel Section
- Orange County Register Travel Section
- Traveling magazines/publications
- Travel bloggers
- Departures
- Condé Nast Traveler
- Condé Nast Travel+Leisure
- Westways
- Good Sam Club, Highways Magazine

National Consumer, In-Flight

- Southwest Airlines, Spirit Magazine
- American Airlines, American Way Magazine
- Delta Airlines, Delta Sky Magazine
- Hemispheres Magazine
- SkyMall Magazine (An Advertising Vehicle)

Markets Surrounding Costco/Central Market Locations

- Los Angeles/Orange County/Inland Empire
- Northern California
- Connecticut
- Delaware
- Hawaii
- Maryland
- Massachusetts
- Nevada
- New Hampshire
- New York
- Pennsylvania
- Texas
- Vermont
- Virginia
- Food and Family bloggers in each market
- Costco Connection

The press kit will be the starting point for Golden Island's voice and messaging. With a unique and long family history, Golden Island has a great story to tell and the press kit will set the theme and tone for that message. The press kit will also make the company human through the biographies of company leadership. Our messaging and theme for Golden Island will revolve around the phrase *Made in America with Flavors from Around the World*, which adds to the mystique and flavor adventure consumers experience when eating Golden Island products. This is a message that will resonate well with many jerky buyers, eaters, and the media.

3. **Strategy**: Client will identify pertinent food distributors and buyers across the country and introduce the Golden Island brand and products to them, setting the stage for meetings with the Golden Island sales team.

   Tactics: Agency will create an attractive brochure and an innovative mailer campaign geared to distributors/buyers with percentages of sales figures and reasons to stock Golden Island products. The mailer will be performed in a two-step process.

   1. Send a creative pitch press release about the new and attractive packaging and announcing the new website.

   2. Send samples of products for distributors and buyers to taste again with a creative pitch letter.

4. **Strategy**: Media have transformed in recent years with the success of social media platforms such as Facebook, Twitter and Pinterest. It is something that is no longer a consideration but a mandatory tool in the field of public relations.

   Tactics: Expand social media presence through a website and Facebook overhaul with regular postings on Facebook and on the Golden Island blog and the addition of a Twitter handle and Pinterest. Place pictures of jerky products and inspiration for jerky such as marinades, smokehouses, or even creative ways people are enjoying beef jerky, i.e., Bloody Marys, salads, while on trips, etc.

   Tools: Agency will draft a weekly Facebook posting sheet with 5–10 engaging posts per week. These posts will not be solely about Golden Island but rather a variety of topics that interest the jerky eater, such as sports, outdoor activities, etc.

   Since March 30, 2012, Facebook has required all brands to follow the "Timeline" format. This change allows the Golden Island page to have a large image as its "Background" and also gives the brand a chance to expand its history beyond the time it has had a Facebook presence going back as far as the company's roots in Taiwan in 1952.

   Agency will also provide information to client about Facebook advertising, which can grow brand followers and the base of customers connected via social media.

   With the client's input, the agency will also draft and edit regular postings to the Golden Island blog. These weekly posts will be a longer version of a topic discussed during the week in a Facebook post.

The agency will create five twitter postings per week, which are short and designed to generate excitement with the brand.

Pinterest is the latest social media outlet to gain considerable notoriety. It is a visual medium that focuses on pictures placed on a virtual "pin board" where users can post images of items they find of interest on the Internet.

The agency will create a Golden Island pin board and send the client 10 photos gained from research online and any copy that should accompany the photos for approval.

5. **Strategy**: Partner with military support groups to establish a positive relationship with this target public.

   Tactics: Agency will research and contact SoCal [Southern California] military bases and military unit family support groups to donate Golden Island product for care packages. The agency will also contact the City of Rancho Cucamonga, as it has a long history of military support and the local connection between the Kans and Golden Island's place of business is a natural fit. Additionally, the agency will look into opportunities to work with groups such as the Wounded Warrior project.

   Tools: Once a group is identified and Golden Island has begun supporting them the agency will contact military publications to bring awareness of the work and support Golden Island is giving the troops and will also work toward gaining product reviews in the publications. Further media relations work will involve contacting Sean Hannity of Fox News, who has helped the Wounded Warrior project in years past. All efforts will be subjects for posts on Golden Island's website and social media platforms.

   Military publications include

   - Military Living
   - Military Magazine
   - Stars and Stripes
   - The Leatherneck
   - Marine Times
   - Soldier's Magazine
   - Navy Times

6. **Strategy**: Golden Island has a distinct focus on the wellbeing of its employees and their communities. Projects such as the Holiday Giving Tree and the efforts to better the lives of those in the surrounding communities are a rarity in business and should be touted.

   Tactics: The agency will use media pitch letters, press releases, and follow-up calls to human interest editors and reporters in the communities where the Golden Island philanthropic efforts are taking place. These philanthropic efforts and media gained from the outreach about philanthropy will also be promoted on Golden Island's social media platforms and website.

7. **Strategy**: With Anna Kan's experience in corporate leadership and devotion to helping people better themselves and her community, she is a perfect fit for speaking engagements to aspiring entrepreneurs, as well as undergraduate and graduate degree students who wish to start their own businesses.

   Tactics: Agency will research speaking engagements in the Inland Empire and surrounding area with Asian, women, and business groups where Anna Kan can attend and speak on her experiences, inspiring others to follow their dreams and callings. This will allow another outlet for Anna Kan to give back to the community while building greater brand recognition for Golden Island.

   Tools: Possible speaking engagement opportunities

   - USC Marshall School of Business, Lloyd Greif Center for Entrepreneurial Studies
   - Entrepreneurship groups
   - University of California, Riverside Anderson Graduate School of Management
   - CSU, Fullerton Mihaylo College of Business and Economics, Center for Entrepreneurship
   - IE area Chambers of Commerce

8. **Possible 2013 Strategy**: Have high-profile chefs cook with Golden Island jerky to gain notoriety as a truly gourmet product.

   Tactics: The agency will research chefs already using jerky and contact them via pitch letters and product samples. The agency will follow up with these chefs to see if they are interested in switching to Golden Island jerky in place of the products they are currently using. If successful, the agency will publicize chefs using Golden Island products in the markets where the chefs live and work.

9. **Possible 2013 Strategy**: In building Golden Island's public relations presence, the agency will actively research and pursue award opportunities, which will bring greater exposure to the brand and its efforts to not only sell jerky but also take an active interest in the wellbeing of employees and their families.

   Tactics: The agency will research award opportunities in both snack trade and the Inland Empire and present to client prior to entering. If Golden Island wins the award competitions entered, the agency will produce and distribute press releases and promote the award recognition on Golden Island's social media platforms and website to bring greater awareness to the Golden Island brand and its status as a leader in the meat snack industry and Inland Empire community.

APPENDIX CHART 9-1: Campaign Timeline Gantt Chart

Activity	Mar	Apr	May	Jun	Jul	Aug	Sep	Oct	Nov	Dec
Create media list	■									
Identify editorial calendar opportunities	■									
Draft and finalize press release		■								
Finalize distributor & buyer marketing program		■								
Begin distributing information										
Identify & dicuss list of award opportunities			■							
Research & present speaking opportunities to client			■							
Finalize product release			■							
Distribute product release to trade & consumer media			■							
Agency pitches all month				■						
Develop 2013 plan						■				
Present research on local military units to receive donations							■			
Contact military media								■		
Contact media re: philanthropy with holiday push									■	
Pitch Giving Tree									■	

1. **Calendar**

   - March: Create media list and identify editorial calendar opportunities.

   - April: Draft and finalize press kit.

   - April: Agency will finalize distributor and buyer marketing program and begin distributing information.

   - May: Agency will begin social media postings and will launch Twitter and Pinterest pages.

   - May: Agency will identify list of award opportunities and discuss which to enter with client and timeline of entry deadlines.

   - May: Agency will research speaking engagements and present to client.

   - May: Finalize product release (specific product or products TBD) and distribute to trade and consumer media; agency will pitch for an entire month after distribution of release.

   - August: Develop 2013 PR plan.

   - September: Agency will present research on which local military units to donate Golden Island product.

   - October: Agency will contact military media to pitch story about donations to military unit.

   - November: Agency will contact media regarding Golden Island philanthropic efforts with a holiday push and pitch surrounding the company's giving tree.

2. **Campaign Budget**

   NOTE: The budget for this plan is proprietary, so the information in Table 9-1 is a partial hypothetical example of a budget format.

C. **Evaluation**

1. The first objective, which is to create brand awareness of Golden Island products with at least 15 food distributors/buyers, will be evaluated by counting the number of distributors/buyers that have accepted the product. In-store distribution of Golden Island Gourmet Jerky products will be assessed by tracking the products distributed and the stores in which distribution took place.

2. The objective to increase brand awareness of Golden Island by 10% with media and consumers on regional and national levels will be measured by pre- and post-campaign surveys.

3. The objective to expand the current distributor and buyer marketing program by 10% will be evaluated by comparing precampaign figures with postcampaign figures.

4. The objective to develop a social media presence for Golden Island by the end of the year will be evaluated by such tracking such things as Facebook "likes," followers, fans, and online comments from the community.

5. The objective to develop brand loyalty and a Golden Island following among military and military families by the end of the year will be evaluated by tracking the number of military support groups that partner with Golden Island and sales at military installations.

6. The objective to enhance the brand's image by highlighting the company's philanthropic efforts will be measured by pre- and postcampaign attitudinal surveys.

7. The objective to position Anna Kan as an expert in business and leadership for speaking engagements, gaining exposure for her and the Golden Island Brand will be evaluated by the number of speaking engagements completed and informal feedback from the audiences.

APPENDIX TABLE 9-1: Campaign Budget

Direct Program Costs	Jan	Feb	Mar	Apr	May	Jun	Totals
Research							
Books (specify titles)	$350						$350
Dues & Subscriptions (specify)	$200						$200
Focus Groups		$2,500					$2,500
Pre-Post Campaign Surveys	$1,250	$0	$0	$0	$0	$1,250	$2,500
Subtotal	*$1,800*	*$2,500*	*$0*	*$0*	*$0*	*$1,250*	*$5,550*
Publicity							
Press Kits	$0	$0	$1,275	$0	$0	$0	$1,275
Mailing Supplies & Postage	$0	$0	$1,200	$0	$0	$0	$1,200
Distribution Service (specify)	$0	$0	$800	$0	$0	$0	$800
Media Monitoring & Clipping Service	$0	$0	$700	$700	$700	$700	$2,800
Printing & Folding × 1,000	$0	$1,500	$0	$0	$0	$0	$1,500
Subtotal	*$0*	*$1,500*	*$3,975*	*$700*	*$700*	*$700*	*$7,575*
Program Total	*$1,800*	*$4,000*	*$3,975*	*$700*	*$700*	*$1,950*	*$13,125*

I. Qualifications

A. **Public Relations Team Members' Duties & Backgrounds**
   The Team

Spend 10 minutes with Melinda Morgan Kartsonis and you'll realize why Morgan Marketing has achieved the success it enjoys today. Sitting at the helm, she leads the charge in building an agency that fosters creativity, communication, and energy. From her personal design of the open offices, to the cheerleader roles she takes with her staff, to her hands-on approach in creativity, it's no wonder she is viewed as passionate, encouraging, and straightforward.

Melinda Morgan Kartsonis, APR, Fellow PRSA
President, Agency Principal

Photo © Lovato Images

Beginning more than 25 years ago working for a prestigious Michigan Avenue PR firm in Chicago, she spent the 1980s honing her craft working for various agencies. Melinda moved on to open Morgan Marketing & PR in 1991. Combining her attention to detail, her ability to develop relationships, and her aggressive, results-oriented approach to marketing communications, she has quickly built a client roster to be proud of.

Melinda has always been active in the community, with an impressive list of board or committee positions for organizations such as City of Hope, St. Joseph Hospital, Orange County Performing Arts Center Business Partnership Alliance, California Restaurant Association of Orange County, American Institute of Wine and Food, the American Cancer Society Corporate Advisory Council, Women's Foodservice Forum, and Les Dames d'Escoffier International. To share her passion for the PR industry, she has also been a faculty member at University of California at Irvine, Chapman University, California State University Fullerton, and California State University Long Beach, and she's served with the Orange County Public Relations Society of America.

She's received the Public Relations Society of America Distinguished Service Award, been included with *Orange Coast* magazine's "Hot 11" in its Power of PR issue, and been named the Orange County's *Business Journal's* "Top Businesswoman"—many times. She has also received awards from the Cystic Fibrosis Foundation (Orange County's Finest) and American Lung Association (Volunteer of the Year).

So what makes Melinda tick? She requires Think Tank time—quiet time alone behind the wheel of her car formulating the next big splash.

Stephen Gregg,
Senior Account
Executive

Photo © Tom Duncan

A Southern California native, Stephen lives by the mantra Work Hard, Play Hard. With a wealth of experience exclusively in agency public relations, Stephen thrives in the fast-paced world of managing multiple clients, meeting critical deadlines, and developing media placements. At Morgan Marketing and Public Relations, LLC, Stephen is responsible for the day-to-day needs of a number of clients, which include strategic planning, implementing communications programs, crafting press releases and collateral materials, pitching stories to a variety of media outlets, fulfilling the social media needs of clients, as well as facilitating the growth of new business.

Prior to joining the team at Morgan Marketing and Public Relations, LLC, Stephen served with Faubel Public Affairs and represented both private companies and public agencies, working on numerous community outreach campaigns throughout Orange County, California. Notably, he led the communications campaign for the victorious "Yes on Measure B" project in San Juan Capistrano, which upheld a city council's decision on property rights. Stephen also has a wealth of experience representing clients in the areas of healthcare, consumer products, architecture, and entertainment.

When Stephen is not in the office, he enjoys traveling, working on his vintage Mustang, and experimenting in the kitchen. He is an Eagle Scout, an avid beachgoer, snowboarder, and outdoorsman.

Stephen is also active as a volunteer with Future Leaders of Our Community, and he is a member of the Public Relations Society of America. He graduated from California State University, Fullerton, with a Bachelor of Arts degree in Communications: Public Relations, and lives in Laguna Niguel.

B. **Reporting Procedures**

At Morgan Marketing & PR, we have small teams of very smart people giving a great deal of concentration to our clients. Every client matters, and our service reflects that. Clients partner with experienced practitioners, not entry-level staff, and our long-term client relationships speak to the success we achieve. Our services are delivered by friendly, focused professionals with strong values and insightful ideas. And, with a specialty in the food and restaurant industry, all our clients benefit from our onsite test kitchen (who doesn't like warm, homemade chocolate chip cookies at their meetings?).

V. Appendix: (Sample Deliverables, Media Lists, Etc., Should Appear Here, As Well As References.)

Primary Research Methods

A link to a questionnaire was posted to Facebook, yielding 120 responses. The questionnaire was composed of the following items:

Open-Ended Questions

1. What is your least favorite thing about jerky?
2. What is your favorite characteristic of jerky?
3. What qualities do you want in jerky?

The responses were tabulated into categories. The most popular two or three are reported in the proposal.

Closed-Ended Questions

7. Do you take jerky with you on the go?   Yes   No
8. Is jerky a good source of protein?   Yes   No
9. Have you heard of Golden Island Jerky? Yes   No
10. Where do you purchase jerky?

    a. Costco
    b. Convenience stores
    c. Markets
    d. Other

11. What are your reasons for eating jerky?

    a. Taste
    b. Convenience
    c. Nutrition
    d. Other

12. What is your gender?   Male   Female
13. What is your age?   18–24   25–39   40–59   60+

References

Agricultural Marketing Resource Center. (2012). *Dried beef industry profile*. Ames, IA: Author. Retrieved from http://www.agmrc.org/commodities__products/livestock/beef/dried_beef_industry_profile.cfm

Clark, S. (2011, March 22). *12 packable muscle-building snacks*. Meridian, ID: BodyBuilding.com. Retrieved from http://www.bodybuilding.com/fun/12-packable-muscle-building-snacks.html

Fredricksen, C. (2012, February 22). *Google edges closer to Facebook as U.S. display advertising becomes two-horse race* [Press release]. New York: eMarketer. Retrieved from http://www.emarketer.com/PressRelease.aspx?R=1008856

Gallup. (2012, March 12–18). *Gallup daily: Politics* [Poll]. Washington, DC: Author. Retrieved from http://www.gallup.com/poll/politics.aspx

Gallup. (2012, March 12–18). *Gallup economy* [Poll]. Washington, DC: Author. Retrieved from http://www.gallup.com/poll/economy.aspx.

Global Industry Analysts, Inc. (2012, January 18). *Global snack foods market to reach US$334.7 by 2015, according to new report by Global Industry Analysts, Inc.* Retrieved from http://www.prweb.com/releases/snack_foods_nut_snacks/microwaveable_snacks/prweb9116978.htm

Goodpurpose. (2010). *The Goodpurpose 4th annual global study*. Retrieved from http://www.goodpurposecommunity.com/pages/globalstudy.aspx#

Kowalski, A., & Chandra, S. (2012). U.S. outlook optimism at eight-year high: Economy. *Bloomberg Businessweek: NewsFromBloomberg*. Retrieved from http://www.businessweek.com/news/2012-03-22/jobless-claims-in-u-dot-s-dot-decline-to-lowest-level-in-four-years

Moats Kennedy, Inc. (2011, October 3). *Demographics: Foodies take a new turn*. Chicago: Author. Retrieved from http://www.moatskennedy.com/2011/10/03/demographics-foodies-take-a-new-turn

Report Buyer. (2009, January). *Foodies in the U.S.: Five cohorts: Foreign/spicy, restaurant, cooks, gourmet and organic/natural* [Market research report]. London: Author. Retrieved from http://www.reportbuyer.com/leisure_media/dining/foodies_u_s_five_cohorts_foreign_spicy_restaurant_cooks_gourmet_organic_natural.html

Schaefer, R. (2012). *Beef jerky manufacturing* [Nielsen consumer panel]. San Antonio: SBDCNet. Retrieved from http://www.sbdcnet.org/small-business-research-reports/beef-jerky-manufacturing

Snack Food Association. (2012, March 16). *The snack report—March 16, 2012.* Arlington, VA: Author. Retrieved from http://www.sfa2.org/news.php?id=62

U.S. Department of Defense. (2010). *Demographics 2010: Profile of the military community.* Washington, DC: Author. Retrieved from http://www.militaryhomefront.dod.mil/12038/Project%20Documents/MilitaryHOMEFRONT/Reports/2010_Demographics_Report.pdf

GLOSSARY

Advertising equivalency Calculates the value of message exposure as if it were paid advertising.

Audiences See *Publics*.

Backgrounders Provide background on an organization, product, or service; usually enclosed in press kits.

Boolean searches The oldest, simplest, and most widely used type of search structure; "and," "or," and "not" operators.

CARS Checklist for evaluating resources Developed by Dr. Robert Harris, examines resources for *Credibility, Accuracy, Reasonableness*, and *Support*.

Closed systems Systems that are entirely self-contained; exchange no resources with the environment.

Connotative words Evoke emotion or associations. For example: "woman" is denotative; "blonde" is connotative.

Content analysis Analyzes texts for pre-defined concepts, words, or phrases.

Corporate advertising Advertising that is processed and purchased in the usual manner, but is intended to enhance public image rather than sell a product or service. Also called *institutional advertising*.

Cost per person Calculates the cost of reaching each member of the target public by dividing all placement expenses by the number of people potentially reached (media impressions).

Counseling A term coined by Edward L. Bernays that encompasses the advisory role that public relations practitioners play for corporate and institutional management.

Defamation Any published or spoken false statement that damages a person's reputation.

Demographics Categorical information about publics, such as gender, income level, education, age, and ethnicity.

Denotative word Represents the dictionary definition. For example: "woman" is denotative; "blonde" is connotative.

Elaboration Likelihood Model of Persuasion (ELM) Developed by Petty and Cacioppo, ELM proposes that a central route to persuasion is reached through strength of argument and sound evidence while a peripheral route to persuasion is reached through elaborating on positive associations.

Equifinality In systems theory, the ability to achieve a particular goal in different ways and from different starting points.

Ethics A value system by which an individual determines what is right or wrong.

Ethos In Aristotle's *Rhetoric*, the credibility of a message's source. For example: a personal reputation as a truthful individual provides strong *ethos* or source credibility.

Executive summary A one- or two-page summary of a lengthy document, such as a public relations proposal.

Fact sheets Documents that resemble news releases, but serve as quick reference tools for reporters; typically present the "who, what, where, why, when, and how" of the news in bullet form.

Feedback Communication from those affected by a communication activity; the receiver/decoder processes a message and encodes/sends the feedback.

Field searches Specify where the words should appear, such as a title or author in a database search or a URL, headers, or links in a Web-based search.

Formal research Often quantitative; uses scientific or social scientific methodology.

Formative research Research to determine how to proceed with a program; measures inputs, such as feasibility studies, audience analyses, and message testing.

Gantt chart A visual representation of a full program schedule, including the start and completion date of every tool and its preparation. First developed by Henry Gantt, it is a widely used standard in project planning. The planned activities are usually listed down the left side, and the calendar is depicted horizontally across the top.

Gatekeeper A filter between source and receivers, and often a secondary audience. For example: newspaper editors, billboard, or moderating computer system administrator.

Generalizability The extent to which the results of a study sample represents an entire population.

Goal A general direction in which the organization wishes to move; something to be accomplished over time.

Homeostasis Balance; self-maintenance of a system.

Implied consent The concept that by posing for a picture taken for "news" purposes, the person implies consent that it will be so used.

Informal research Does not conform to stringent rules of scientific research; usually qualitative methods, using "soft" data.

Inverted pyramid Traditional structure for news releases in which most important information is placed first.

Issues management Making strategic and tactical decisions on the basis of economic, political, social, and technological forces that impinge on the organization.

Key message A single, declarative sentence that describes a core idea to be conveyed in a message and a short list (no more than three or four items) of supporting information.

Keyword in Context (KWIC) searches Define the context in which the search terms should appear by specifying words that appear near your primary search terms.

Letter of transmittal Accompanies a written document that is being transmitted and describes the general nature of that document. The letter of transmittal introduces the document to the recipient.

Libel A form of defamation; any published, written, false statement that damages a person's reputation.

Logos In Aristotle's *Rhetoric*, a logical argument.

Marketing Focuses on building and maintaining an organization's markets for products or services.

Marketing public relations Supports marketing and sales objectives of the business; often called *marketing communications* or *marcom*

Media impressions Measure the number of individuals who have potentially been exposed to a message based on circulation, viewership, or listenership.

News release A brief document that disseminates news in ready-to-publish form.

Newsworthiness The extent to which media will publish a message. Criteria for newsworthiness include prominence, timeliness, proximity, impact, conflict, and novelty.

Nominal group technique First proposed in 1971 by André L. Delbecq and Andrew H. Van de Ven. This approach facilitates open discussion and encourages equal contributions from all group members.

Nonprobability sample A nonrandom sample, often because either time or logistics dictate a particular group from which population members will be selected.

Objective Target accomplishment that supports a goal and evaluates progress toward it. Motivational objectives should be SMART: *specific, measurable, achievable, relevant,* and *time bound.*

One-Way Asymmetrical Model of Communication Uses persuasion and manipulation to influence and control target publics; also known as the *Press Agentry Model.*

One-Way Symmetrical Model of Communication Differs from the Press Agentry model in that truth and accuracy are important; however, the information is selectively disseminated. Often called the *Public Information Model.*

Open systems Exchange resources with the environment.

Operationalization Defines a phenomenon in such a way that it is observable and measurable.

Opinion leaders Individuals who are knowledgeable and articulate on issues of interest to the public serve as catalysts for opinion formation.

Pathos In Aristotle's *Rhetoric,* an emotional appeal.

PEST Analysis Analyzes environmental Political, Economic, Sociological, and Technological influences on an organization.

Phrase searches Use phrases as a default or by delineating the phrase with quotation marks, such as "teddy bear."

Position statements State organizational positions on issues or policies.

Press agentry Usually tied to celebrity public relations, the promotion of celebrities, books, events, or other clients through shrewd use of media. Often associated with the tactics of P. T. Barnum.

Press kits Usually consist of large pocket folders that contain extensive information in ways that provide flexibility and ease-of-access to media.

Primary publics The people a public relations professional is trying to influence.

Primary research Based on raw data collected by the researcher, such as original survey studies.

Probability sample A sample in which every member of the population has an equal chance of being selected. Example: a *random sample.*

Professional associations Organizations in which members are individuals who are involved in a profession or skilled craft, organized for mutual benefit (for example: PRSA; American Medical Association).

Proximity searches Similar to *KWIC searches*; indicate the range of words within which the contextual word appears.

Psychographics Categorical information about a public's lifestyles, attitudes, values, and beliefs.

Publics Groups of people or organizations that may affect an organization.

Publicity A subspecialty of public relations; information disseminated through mass media to attract favorable public notice.

Pyramid Model of PR Research Designed by Dr. Jim Macnamara, categorizes public relations research in terms of Inputs, Outputs, and Outcomes.

Qualitative research Involves "soft" data concerning such information as people's experiences and values.

Quantitative research Involves numerical measures and yields "hard" data.

Random sample A sample in which every member of the population has an equal chance of being selected; also known as *probability sample.*

Reliability The extent to which a particular method will repeatedly yield the same results when used to measure the same phenomena over time.

Return on Investment (ROI) The extent to which the resources invested in a program will result in a net gain or loss.

Secondary public A group or individual who can influence primary publics in some way.

Secondary research Drawn from material that is archived by others, such as databases and library materials.

Self-regulation and control The ways in which systems regulate their behavior to achieve their goals.

Situation analysis Investigates the current situation of a client, both internally and externally. May include a PEST analysis and/or SWOT analysis.

Situational theory Developed by James Grunig, identifies audiences as active or passive.

Slander A form of defamation; any spoken, false statement that damages a person's reputation.

Smart news releases Provide online content in multiple formats, including multimedia, and enable immediate download for a variety of media outlet platforms.

Source credibility Refers to the extent to which audience members perceive the message source as knowledgeable, objective, and honest about a given subject.

Social media news releases Provide online content specifically designed to encourage interactivity, such as blogs, RSS feeds, bookmarking, and the like.

Strategy Overall concept that unifies and propels tactics into a cohesive program to attain stated objectives.

Subsystem A system that is also a component of a larger suprasystem.

Suprasystem A system in which the components are smaller subsystems.

Summative research Used to evaluate the success of a program and measure outcomes.

SWOT Analysis Analyzes the Strengths, Weaknesses, Opportunities, and Threats of an organization.

System theory A broad approach to communication, largely borrowed from biological sciences, which focuses on the interrelatedness of system components.

Systems Entities that are formed by sets of things that relate to one another to form a unique whole. Generally, systems are characterized by: (1) objects (components, parts, elements, or variables of the system); (2) attributes (qualities of the system and its components); (3) internal relationships between the components, and (4) environment (the system's surroundings).

Synergy Components or agents come together to create a magnified outcome.

Tactics Specific approaches; when, where, how to complete objectives; may include multiple tools.

Team According to Katzenbach and Smith, "a small group of people with complementary skills who are committed to a common purpose, performance goals and approaches for which they are held mutually accountable."

Team Life Cycle Forming, storming, norming, performing, and adjourning.

Tools Specific channels used to communicate with target publics.

Truncation searches Allow the use of "wild card" characters to complete a search term that has many variations.

Two-Way Asymmetrical Model of Communication Based on social scientific theories and methods, including research; sometimes called *scientific persuasion*. Practitioners both gather information from and provide it to target publics, using social scientific methods.

Two-Way Symmetrical Model of Communication Relies on social scientific research methods and emphasizes a true dialog between organizations and their publics.

Validity The extent to which the research measures are appropriate for the phenomenon in question. For example: A researcher wishes to determine how caffeine intake affects alertness, and decides to measure how much individuals talk within an hour after drinking two cups of coffee. This study would not be valid, because the research is really measuring verbosity, not alertness. A more valid measure might be reaction times or other physiological measures.

BIBLIOGRAPHY

AccuConference. (n.d.). *Undeniable conference impact: Using visual aids.* Henderson, NV: Author. Retrieved from http://www.accuconference.com/resources/conference-impact.aspx

Aldrich, H. & Herker, D. (1977). Boundary spanning roles and organization structure. *The Academy of Management Review, 2*(2), 217–230.

Alessandra, T., & O'Connor, M. J. (1996). *The platinum rule.* New York: Warner Brooks.

Anderson, F. W., Hadley, L., Rockland, D., & Weiner, M. (2009). *Guidelines for setting measurable public relations objectives: An update* [Whitepaper]. Gainesville, FL: The Institute for Public Relations, Commission on PR Measurement and Evaluation. Retrieved from http://www.instituteforpr.org/wp-content/uploads/Setting_PR_Objectives.pdf

Aristotle. (c. 335–323 BCE). *The metaphysics* (Book VIII, Part 6). New York: Cosimo.

Aristotle, & Freese, J. (1959). *The "Art" of Rhetoric.* Cambridge, Mass.: Harvard University Press

Athey, T. H. (1982). *Systematic systems approach: An integrated method for solving systems problems.* Englewood Cliffs, NJ: Prentice-Hall.

Babbie, E. R. (2010). *The practice of social research.* Belmont, CA: Wadsworth.

Bandura, A. (2000). Exercise of human agency through collective-efficacy. *Current Directions in Psychological Science, 9*(3), 75–78.

Bernays, E. L. (1929). *Crystallizing public opinion.* New York: Liveright.

von Bertalanffy, L. (1968). *General systems theory.* New York: Braziller.

Blumer, R., & Moyers, B. (1984). *A walk through the twentieth century with Bill Moyers: The image makers* [video]. College Park, MD: Corporation for Entertainment & Learning, Inc.

Centers for Disease Control and Prevention (CDC). (2011). *Emergency Preparedness and Response.* Retrieved from http://www.bt.cdc.gov/socialmedia/zombies.asp

Cutlip, S. M., Center, A. H., & Broom, G. M. (1994). *Effective public relations.* Englewood Cliffs, NJ: Prentice-Hall.

De'Alesio, R. (2011, September). Centers for Disease Control and Prevention: Preparedness 101: Zombie apocalypse. In *PRNews Platinum PR Awards Issue.* Retrieved from http://www.prnewsonline.com/download/G45318_AI-PBI_PRN_Platinum_Issue_2011.pdf

Delbecq, A. L., & Van de Ven, A. H. (1971). A group process model for problem identification and program planning. *Journal of Applied Behavioral Science, VII.* 466–491.

Devine, D. J., & Clayton, L. D. (1999). Teams in organizations. *Small Group Research, 30*(6), 678–712.

Diehl, M., & Stroebe, W. (1987). Productivity loss in brainstorming groups: Toward the solution of a riddle. *Journal of Personality and Social Psychology, 53*(3), 497–509.

Doran, G. T. (1981). There's a S.M.A.R.T. way to write management's goals and objectives. *Management Review, 70*(11), 35–36.

Drucker, P. F. (1954). *The practice of management.* New York: HarperCollins.

Escobar, J. F. (2008). Public relations agency compensation: *Enhancing value through best practices.* Retrieved from http://prfirms.org/resources/public-relations-agency-compensation-enhancing-value-through-best-practices

Fast Horse. (2011). *Fast Horse and Coke Engage the World.* Retrieved from http://fasthorseinc.com/home/fast-horse-portfolio/clients/coca-cola/expedition206

Fast Horse & The Coca-Cola Company. (2011). *Coca-Cola's expedition 206.* Retrieved from http://www.prsa.org/SearchResults/Download/6BE-1102C07

Friedman, M. (1975, December 7). *Richard Heffner's Open Mind* [Television Interview Program]. New York: WNET.

Fritz, J. (2010, February 22). *Using social media to win charity competitions: How email trumped social media for Kiwanis in the Chase Giving Contest.* Retrieved from http://nonprofit.about.com/od/fundraising/a/kiwanisandchase.htm

Geisel, T. S. (Dr. Seuss). (1975). *Oh, the thinks you can think!* New York: Random House.

Goncalo, J., Polman, E., & Maslach, C. (2010). Can confidence come too soon? Collective efficacy, conflict and group performance over time. *Organizational Behavior & Human Decision Processes, 113*(1), 13–24.

Greater Houston Convention and Visitors Bureau. (2011). *Houston culinary tours.* Public Relations Society of America Silver Anvil Awards. Retrieved from http://www.prsa.org/SearchResults/Download/6BW-1102D01

Grunig, J. E. (Ed.). (1992). *Excellence in public relations and communication.* Hillsdale, NJ: Lawrence Erlbaum Associates.

Grunig, J. E. (1997). A situational theory of publics: Conceptual history, recent challenges and new research. In D. Moss, T. MacManus, & D. Vercic (Eds.), *Public relations research: An international perspective.* (pp. 3–48). London: International Thomson Business Press.

Grunig, J. E., & Hunt, T. (1984). *Managing public relations*. New York: Holt, Rinehart & Winston.

Grunig, L. A., Grunig, J. E., & Dozier, D. M. (2002). *Excellent public relations and effective organizations: A study of communication management in three countries*. Mahwah, NJ: Lawrence Erlbaum Associates.

Hallahan, K. (2004). Exhibit 7: Campaigns budget reminder checklist. *Communication campaign/Program organizer*. Retrieved from http:/lamar.colostate.edu/~pr/organizer5.pdf

Harris, R. D. (2012). *The CARS Checklist for information quality*. Retrieved from http://www.virtualsalt.com/evalu8it.htm

Hays, B. A., & Swanson, D. J. (2011). Prevalence and success of reverse mentoring in public relations. *Public Relations Journal, 5*(4), 1–18.

Hill and Knowlton & Johnson & Johnson. (2011). *text4baby going mobile with pregnancy education*. Retrieved from http://www.pisa.org/SearchResults/view/6BW-1105D05/0/text4baby_Going_Mobile_with_Pregnancy_Education

Kalmar, B., Ruby, H., Sheekman, A., & Perrin, N. (1933). *Duck Soup*. Internet Movie Database. Retrieved from http://www.imdb.com/title/tt0023969

Katzenbach, J. R., & Smith, D. K. (1993). The discipline of teams. *Harvard Business Review, 71*(March–April), 111–146.

Kent, M. L., & Taylor, M. (2002). Toward a dialogic theory of public relations. *Public Relations Review, 28*, 21–37.

Lasswell, H. D. (1948). *Power and personality*. New York: W. W. Norton.

Ledingham, J. A., & Bruning, S. D. (Eds.). (2000). *Public relations as relationship management: A relational approach to the study and practice of public relations*. Mahwah, NJ: Lawrence Erlbaum Associates.

Macnamara, J. R. (2011, December 9). PR metrics. *Whitepaper for International Association for the Measurement and Evaluation of Communication*. Retrieved from http://amecorg.com/wp-content/uploads/2011/10/PR-Metrics-Paper.pdf

Macnamara, J. (2002). Research and evaluation. In C. Tymson & P. Lazar, *The New Australian and New Zealand Public Relations Manual* (pp. 100–134). Sydney: Tymson Communications.

Malloy, J. T. (1988). *John T. Malloy's new dress for success*. New York: Warner Books.

Miyamoto, C. T. (n.d.). *How to write a comprehensive public relations plan*. Retrieved from http://www.hotwireprc.com/documents/How%20To%20Write%20A%20Comprehensive%20Public%20Relations%20Plan.pdf

Moriarty, S. E. (1997). The big idea: Creativity in public relations. In C. L. Caywood (Ed.), *The handbook of strategic public relations and integration* (pp. 554–563). New York: McGraw-Hill.

Nager, N. R., & Allen, T. H. (1984). *Public relations management by objectives.* New York: Longman.

Nankivell, F. (1906, May 23). *The infant Hercules and the Standard Oil serpents.* Washington, DC: Library of Congress, Prints and Photographs division. Retrieved from http://www.theodorerooseveltcenter.org/Research/Digital-Library/Record.aspx?libID=o278539

National Association of Colleges and Employers. (2011, November). *Job outlook 2012.* Bethelehem, PA: Author. Retrieved from http://www.naceweb.org/job_outlook_2012

OneVoice & Philips Norelco. (2011). *Philips Norelco Deforest Yourself, Reforest the World.* Retrieved from http://www.prsa.org/SearchResults/view/6BW-1103A32/0/Philips_Norelco_Deforest_Yourself_Reforest_the_Wor

Parise, S., & Rollag, K. (2010). Emergent network structure and initial group performance: The moderating role of pre-existing relationships. *Journal of Organizational Behavior, 31*(6), 877–897.

PepsiCo & Edelman and Weber Shandwick. (2011). *Pepsi refresh project.* Public Relations Society of America Silver Anvil Awards. Retrieved from http://www.prsa.org/SearchResults/Download/6BW-1101A05

Petty, R. E., & Cacioppo, J. T. (1981). *Attitudes and persuasion: Classic and contemporary approaches.* Dubuque, IA: Wm. C. Brown.

Petty, R. E., & Cacioppo, J. T. (1986). *Communication and persuasion: Central and peripheral routes to attitude change.* New York: Springer-Verlag.

Picasso, P. (n.d.). BrainyQuote.com. Retrieved from http://www.brainyquote.com/quotes/authors/p/pablo_picasso_3.html

Pollard, W. (n.d.). Great-Quotes.com. Retrieved from http://www.great-quotes.com/quote/201010

Pyle, K. (2005). Youth are the present. *Telephony, 246,* 40. Cited in B. A. Hays & D. J. Swanson. (2011). Prevalence and success of reverse mentoring in public relations. *Public Relations Journal, 5*(4, 17).

Rector, L. H. (2008). Comparison of Wikipedia and other encyclopedias for accuracy, breadth, and depth in historical articles. *Reference Services Review, 36*(1), 7–22.

Reinhardt, A. (1998, May). Steve Jobs: 'There's sanity returning.' *BusinessWeek.* Retrieved from http://www.businessweek.com/1998/21/b3579165.htm

Rice On-line Writing Lab. (n.d.). *Designing effective oral presentations*. Henderson, NV: AccuConference. Retrieved from http://www.accuconference.com/resources/conference-impact.aspx

Schramm, W. (1954). How communication works. In W. Schramm (Ed.), *The process and effects of mass communication*. Urbana, IL: University of Illinois Press.

Shannon, C. E., & Weaver, W. (1949). *The mathematical theory of communication*. Urbana, IL: University of Illinois Press. (Reprinted with corrections from *The Bell System Technical Journal*, *27*, (July, October, 1948), 379–423, 623–656)

Sledzik, W. E. (2008, August 10). *The '4 models' of public relations practice: How far have you evolved?* [Blog]. Retrieved from http://et.kent.edu/toughsledding/?p=969

South Wales Fire & Rescue Service. (2011). *Project Bernie*. Chartered Institute of Public Relations Excellence Awards. Retrieved from http://www.cipr.co.uk/sites/default/files/Project%20Bernie.pdf

Starbucks Coffee Company & Edelman. (2011). *Starbucks Coffee Company earth month*. Retrieved from http://www.prsa.org/SearchResults/Download/6BE-1107E03

Stohl, C. (1995). *Organizational communication: Connectedness in action*. Thousand Oaks, CA: SAGE Publications.

Texas Commission on the Arts. (n.d.). *Tool-kit*. Austin: Author. Retrieved from http://www.arts.state.tx.us/toolkit/advocacy/templates/key.pdf

text4baby going mobile with pregnancy education. (2011). Retrieved February 15, 2011 from PRSA.org: http://www.prsa.org/SearchResults/view/6BW-1105D05/0/text4baby_Going_Mobile_with_Pregnancy_Education

Thomas, B. (1998, September 9). Babe Ruth quotation in *Congressional Record*, V. 144, Pt. 14, September 9, 1998 to September 21, 1998, p. 19813.

Toastmasters International. (n.d.). *Need help giving a speech?* Retrieved from http://www.toastmasters.org/MainMenuCategories/FreeResources/NeedHelpGivingaSpeech.aspx

Tolkien, J. R. R. (1937). *The Hobbit*. London: Allen & Unwin.

Tuckman, B. W. (1965). Developmental sequence in small groups. *Psychological Bulletin*, *63*, 384–399. (Reprinted in *Group Facilitation: A Research and Applications Journal*, *3*, 66–81. Retrieved from ABI/INFORM Global [Document ID: 353167091]).

Tuckman, B. W., & Jensen, M. A. (1977). Stages of small-group development revisited. *Group & Organization Studies*, *2*(4), 419–427.

Undeniable conference impact: Using visual aids. (n.d.). Henderson, NV: AccuConference. Retrieved from http://www.accuconference.com/resources/conference-impact.aspx

Watson, T., & Noble, P. (2007). *Evaluating public relations: A best practice guide to public relations planning, research and evaluation.* Philadelphia: Kogan Page.

INDEX

A

Accidental sampling, 80
Active publics and persuasion, 58–59
Adjourning stage, team development, 24
Advertising equivalency, 121
Advertising ethics, principles and practices for, 165
American Marketing Association
    ethical norms for marketers, 161
    ethical values for marketers
        citizenship, 163
        fairness, 162
        honesty, 161
        respect, 162
        responsibility, 161–162
        transparency, 163
    implementation of code of ethics of, 163
    preamble, 161
Anderson, Forrest W., 92
Annotated public relations proposal
    campaign budget, 209, 210
    campaign timeline Gantt chart, 208–209
    evaluation of, 209–210
    introduction part, 195
    qualification of PR team members
        duties and backgrounds, 211–212
        reporting procedures, 212
    situation analysis
        PEST analysis, 195–196
        primary research, 197
        SWOT analysis, 196–197
    target audiences, 198–199
    work statement implementation strategy
        consumer outlets outreach, 201–205
        corporate leadership, 207
        creative writing and interviews, 200
        food distributors and buyers, 205
        partnering with military support groups, 206
        pitch publications, 201–202
        possible 2013 strategy, 207
        press releases, 201
        social media marketing, 205–206
    work statement planning
        goals & SMART objectives, 199
        key messages, 199
The Arthur W. Page Society, 10
Art role in people's lives, 98–99
Attitude of team, managing, 26
Audience analysis
    in PR plan development, 43–44
    tactics selection, 107–108
Audiences, active and passive, difference between, 58

B

Balanced scale questionnaire, 84
Barnum, P. T., 7
Bernays, Edward L., 8
"Big Idea" development and persuasion, 59–61
Bodygrooming product campaign, planning checklist for, 99–100
Boolean search, 75
Brainstorming, 60–61
Brand awareness, creating and increasing, 179–183
Brand loyalty, developing, 184–185
Brand's image, enhancing, 185
Budget section of PR plan
    checklist of items to include in, 110–112
    content of, 112
    guideline for writing, 110
    hypothetical format for, 112–113
    rationale for expenditures, 109
Business communicators, IABC Code of Ethics for, 157–159
Business goals
    general categories of, 92
    and productivity, relation between, 92–93
Buyers and sellers, balancing needs of, 162

C

Truncation searches, 75

Twitter postings, 184, 206

Two-way communication models
based on social scientific theories, 8
normative model, 9

Two-way symmetrical model of communication. *See* Normative model

U

Unbalanced scale questionnaire, 84

U.S. Centers for Disease Control and Prevention
campaign for emergency preparedness, 106–107

V

Van de Ven, Andrew H., 61

Visual aids
key to successful, 144
planning, 142
technology usage in, 142
"three Bs" of, 142–144

W

Weaver, Warren, 4–5

Weiner, Mark, 92

Wikipedia, accuracy rate of, 77

Wilbur Schramm mode of communication, 5–6

Women-owned business publications, increasing brand awareness using, 180, 201

Work ethics of team, 22–23

Work proposal. *See* Proposal

Work statement
final report, 132
implementation strategy, Golden Island Gourmet Jerky PR proposal
consumer outlets outreach, 202–205
corporate leadership, 207
creative writing and interviews, 200
food distributors and buyers, 205
partnering with military support groups, 206
pitch publications, 201–202
possible 2013 strategy, 207
press releases, 201
social media marketing, 205–206
planning, Golden Island Gourmet Jerky PR proposal
goals & SMART objectives, 199
key messages, 199
of proposal, 48